EDITED BY
IRENE HARDILL, JURGEN GROTZ AND
LAURA CRAWFORD

MOBILISING VOLUNTARY ACTION IN THE UK

Learning from the Pandemic

T0313621

POLICY PRESS SHORTS POLICY & PRACTICE

First published in Great Britain in 2022 by

Policy Press, an imprint of
Bristol University Press
University of Bristol
1–9 Old Park Hill
Bristol
BS2 8BB
UK
t: +44 (0)117 374 6645
e: bup-info@bristol.ac.uk

Details of international sales and distribution partners are available at
policy.bristoluniversitypress.co.uk

British Library Cataloguing in Publication Data
A catalogue record for this book is available from the British Library

ISBN 978-1-4473-6722-2 paperback
ISBN 978-1-4473-6723-9 OA ePub
ISBN 978-1-4473-6724-6 OA ePdf

Cover design: Bristol University Press
Front cover image: Brendan Gallagher - brendangallagher.net
Printed and bound by CPI Group (UK) Ltd, Croydon, CR0 4YY

This book is dedicated to the volunteers from across the UK who 'made a difference', and those organisations who helped volunteers to support others to get through the pandemic. Thank you.

Contents

List of figures, tables and images   vii

List of abbreviations   viii

Notes on contributors   ix

Acknowledgements   xiii

Foreword   xv
Jurgen Grotz, Eddy Hogg, Véronique Jochum and Ewen Speed

one   Researching in a pandemic   1
Laura Crawford, Irene Hardill and Jurgen Grotz

two   Voluntary action and the pandemic across the UK   19
Ewen Speed, Laura Crawford and Alasdair Rutherford

three   England   40
Eddy Hogg, Joanna Stuart, Amy McGarvey and Catherine Goodall

four   Northern Ireland   61
Denise Hayward, Nick Acheson, Andrew Hanna and Martina McKnight

five   Scotland   81
Matthew Linning and Debbie Maltman

six   Wales   105
James Lundie, Sally Rees and Rhys Dafydd Jones

seven   The road(s) to recovery? Discussion and conclusion   128
           Laura Crawford, Irene Hardill and Jurgen Grotz

Glossary   146

References   158

Index   175

List of figures, tables and images

Figures

2.1	Number of volunteer registrations	30
2.2	Proportion of disabled volunteers	33
4.1	Changes in volunteering responses in Northern Ireland	69
5.1	Scottish COVID-19 timeline	84
5.2	Routemap to Improvement: A Learning Journey	97

Tables

1.1	Pandemic timelines across the UK nations	6
6.1	Different typologies of voluntary activity during the pandemic in Wales	114

Images

1.1	'The Arches' project delivered by Rhayader and District Community Support in Powys, 2020	1
2.1	Volunteer Bikers NI delivering prescriptions in Northern Ireland	19
3.1	A Royal Voluntary Service volunteer at a vaccination centre in England	40
4.1	Volunteers creating food parcels in Belfast, with Belfast City Council, British Red Cross and SOS Bus	61
5.1	Volunteer Edinburgh's Community Taskforce volunteers	81
6.1	Clwb Rygbi Nant Conwy	105
7.1	Embracing living with COVID-19	128

List of abbreviations

CCNI	Charity Commission Northern Ireland
CVC	County Voluntary Council
ESRC	Economic and Social Research Council
LA	local authority
LGA	Local Government Association
NCVO	National Council for Voluntary Organisations
NHSE/I	NHS England and NHS Improvement
NI	Northern Ireland
NVC	National Voluntary Sector Coordination
RVS	Royal Voluntary Service
SAGE	Scientific Advisory Group for Emergencies
SCVO	Scottish Council for Voluntary Organisations
SHS	Scottish Household Survey
SNP	Scottish National Party
TSI	Third Sector Interface
TSO	third sector organisation
TSPC	Third Sector Partnership Council
UK	United Kingdom of Great Britain and Northern Ireland
UKRI	UK Research and Innovation
VCO	voluntary and community organisation
VCS	voluntary and community sector
VIO	volunteer involving organisation
VSSN	Voluntary Sector Studies Network
WCVA	Wales Council for Voluntary Action

Notes on contributors

Nick Acheson is an independent researcher and was formerly Lecturer in Social Policy at Ulster University, Visiting Research Fellow at the Centre for Social Innovation, Trinity College Dublin and editor of *Voluntary Sector Review*. His research has focused on the intersection of social policy and voluntary action in the UK, Ireland and Canada. He has recently completed a comparative analysis of civil society across the EU and in Russia. He is a member of the Board of Volunteer Now.

Laura Crawford is Teaching Fellow at the University of Birmingham. Her research and teaching expertise is in social, cultural and historical geography, specifically focusing on disability, care, research methods and voluntary action.

Catherine Goodall is Senior Policy and Influencing Advisor at the National Council for Voluntary Organisations. Catherine leads on volunteering policy, engaging with a wide range of issues for volunteering. She has a background in supporting systems change in local authorities, research and policy, primarily for children's social care.

Jurgen Grotz is Director of the Institute for Volunteering Research at the University of East Anglia. He is a social scientist and examines the difference volunteering makes to individuals and communities.

Andrew Hanna has been a member of the team at Volunteer Now since September 2018. He has worked with many volunteer involving organisations to help create, improve and adapt their volunteering programmes. He has experience of working with volunteers across a range of settings.

Irene Hardill is Professor of Public Policy, Northumbria University. Her research focuses on volunteering and the voluntary and community sector employing participatory methods. She has recently completed an Economic and Social Research Council-funded study 'Discourses of voluntary action at two "transformational moments" of the welfare state, the 1940s and 2010s' (ES/N018249/1), and "an evaluation of the impact of COVID-19 on methodological innovation: an analysis of ESRC/UKRI social science research projects (July 2020 – July 2021)".

Denise Hayward is Chief Executive of Volunteer Now, the regional volunteering support organisation for Northern Ireland. She has extensive experience in organisational and public volunteering policy development, creating good quality volunteer opportunities and involving volunteers. She has expertise in third sector governance, gained over her career in the voluntary sector.

Eddy Hogg is Senior Lecturer in Social Policy at the University of Kent. His research looks at volunteering, charitable giving and public attitudes to the voluntary sector. Recently he has worked on research on youth volunteering, volunteering in public services, voluntary action for schools, and charity and fundraising regulation.

Véronique Jochum, formerly Head of Research at National Council for Voluntary Organisations, is a freelance social research consultant. Much of her research has looked at volunteering and social action in a range of organisational and community contexts. She has recently worked on a project on inclusive volunteering and disability.

Rhys Dafydd Jones is a social geographer based at Aberystwyth University. He is interested in faith, migration and participation in civil society.

Matthew Linning is Head of Research and Evaluation at Volunteer Scotland. He has published widely on the impact of volunteering participation in society, including the historic environment, youth volunteering, and volunteering health and wellbeing benefits. Formerly he was a Director of DTZ plc heading up its UK Economics Team.

James Lundie is Research Officer at Wales Council for Voluntary Action (WCVA) as well as working in their Grants Team. James was involved in the implementation of the Wales Voluntary Services Emergency and Recovery Funds that supported voluntary organisations during the COVID-19 pandemic. While at WCVA he completed a master's in Social & Public Policy at Cardiff University.

Debbie Maltman is Research Officer at Volunteer Scotland. She has published several reports on volunteering in Scotland, primarily focusing on quantitative analysis and considering different measures of volunteer participation. Prior to joining Volunteering Scotland Debbie undertook a master's in Data Science at Stirling University.

Amy McGarvey is Research Manager at the National Council for Voluntary Organisations. Amy leads on a range of research programmes, including the Time Well Spent series. She has a background in developing and evaluating educational programmes, and spent several years providing research and consultancy to UK policy-makers as a qualitative researcher at TNS BMRB (now Kantar Public).

Martina McKnight is Research Fellow with ARK, Northern Ireland's Social Policy hub. ARK is based across Queen's University Belfast and Ulster University. She is primarily involved with the Young Life and Times and Kids' Life and Times public attitude surveys. Her research interests include gender, young people, conflict and transition in Northern Ireland and qualitative methods.

Sally Rees is Health and Social Care Manager at Wales Council for Voluntary Action and is currently on a two-year secondment to the Welsh Government as Head of Evaluation and New Models of Care. Her research background is in social policy.

Alasdair Rutherford is Professor of Social Statistics in the Faculty of Social Sciences at the University of Stirling. An economist by training, his research focus is on the analysis of administrative and survey data in the fields of volunteering, charity regulation, and risk and resilience in the third sector.

Ewen Speed is Professor of Medical Sociology in the School of Health and Social Care at the University of Essex. He has published on the politics and governance of the English NHS and wider comparative analyses of international health policy. He is associate editor of the journal *Critical Public Health*.

Joanna Stuart is an independent researcher specialising in volunteering and the voluntary sector. Recent work includes research on volunteer wellbeing and the impacts of COVID-19 on voluntary and community organisations. She is a Research Associate at National Council for Voluntary Organisations and Visiting Research Fellow at Nottingham Trent University.

Acknowledgements

This book and the research that underpins it would not have been possible without the generous support of many others including other members of the research team: Alex Farrow, Cathy Hynds, Gemma Jackson, Rahel Spath; data partners Be Collective, Team Kinetic; Advisory Panel members: Georgina Brewis (University College London), Paul Chaney (Wales Institute of Social and Economic Research and Data), Sally Dyson (National Association of Voluntary Services Managers), Angela Ellis Paine (Third Sector Research Centre, Voluntary Sector Studies Network), Sarah Latto (Scottish Volunteering Forum), Ruth Leonard (Association of Volunteer Managers), Sarah Mills (Loughborough University), Wendy Osborne (formerly Volunteer Now), Colin Rochester (Voluntary Action History Society), Baroness Scott of Needham Market, Allison Smith (Royal Voluntary Service), Ian Stevenson (Gateshead Council), Claire Thomas (Bevan Foundation), Chris Wade (Network of National Volunteer-Involving Agencies) and Paul Wilson (Volunteer Edinburgh). We acknowledge the Scottish Government's Third Sector Unit and Resilient Communities Team, the Scottish Council for Voluntary Organisations, the Office of the Scottish Charity Regulator and the TSI Scotland Network for their diverse and invaluable contributions to the research work in Scotland. We are also grateful to our colleagues at Northumbria University, Aberystwyth University, University of East Anglia, University of Kent, University of Essex, University of Stirling and University of Birmingham;

National Council for Voluntary Organisations, Volunteer Now, Volunteer Scotland and Wales Council for Voluntary Action; and our research participants. The research underpinning this book was funded by the Economic and Social Research Council as part of the UK Research and Innovation rapid response COVID-19 call 'Get funding for ideas that address COVID-19', grant reference: ES/V015281/1 – Mobilising voluntary action in the four UK jurisdictions: Learning from today, prepared for tomorrow.

The views expressed are those of the authors alone.

Foreword

Jurgen Grotz, Eddy Hogg,
Véronique Jochum and Ewen Speed

We are writing this foreword on 27 January 2022, the last formal day of a project supported by the Economic and Social Research Council that funded the research which underpins this book, looking back at how this work began, what it was like to work during it and reflect on how it is ending. We are writing it with some trepidation, while COVID-19 cases are again rising.

On 3 April 2020, Eddy Hogg sent an email to a group of colleagues he had just collaborated with a few weeks before:

Hello health volunteering comrades,

I hope you are all coping ok in the current situation. Social isolation is horrid, yet I know I have it far easier than many of you! … Wondered if there was opportunity for a short and sharp bit of research on how the different approaches are working in terms of delivering and mobilising volunteers on the ground.

[Eddy Hogg]

Only days later, a first proposal had been drafted by Jurgen Grotz and reviewed by colleagues, showing how eager we all were to capture what was going on in a systematic way, and to gain new insights. There was so much we didn't understand. We were also desperate to try and help to learn from all this, to be able to 'do our bit'. Yet, no one in the then still quite small writing team could have imagined that nearly two years on, the COVID-19 pandemic still rules much of our lives and that the learning has only just begun.

Cast your mind back to April 2020. Most of us were housebound in social isolation, bewildered and feeling frustrated and helpless. So, we were pleased when we found out that a rolling programme to 'Get funding for ideas that address COVID-19' had been opened by the research funder UK Research and Innovation (UKRI). As researchers interested in volunteering it was clear from the outset that we wanted to collaborate with our colleagues in voluntary and community sector organisations. Véronique Jochum, at that time Head of Research at the National Council for Voluntary Organisations, who had also received Eddy's initial email, became a key conduit for this. Now with Irene Hardill at the helm and Laura Crawford helping, a frantic effort ensued to design a compelling proposal. It is worth remembering that online meetings were not the norm then and boundaries were stretched well beyond the reasonable, as we all had to work from home anyway. Several weekends were spent in front of screens in meetings that were only closed when everybody was just too exhausted to continue.

It was at that stage that the project expanded. While writing the proposal we were listening to the announcements from Whitehall which suggested a unified UK response. Yet, we knew from previous research, especially by Irene Hardill and colleagues, that these were issues relating to devolved powers. Therefore, we reached out to academic and voluntary and community sector colleagues in all four nations of the UK. A comment from one of the future collaborators encapsulates how important this was: "It's just great that somebody actually wants to know what it is like here." But we went further than that and reached out to many key stakeholders who we knew would be able to help us deliver such a complex project. For our data collection plans it was a great relief when the digital platform operators Team Kinetic and Be Collective unbureaucratically agreed that they would share some of their anonymised user data for this critical period. Their positive approach to sharing that data and making a difference at such a challenging time is testament to the social commitment of these organisations.

We were delighted that colleagues from other universities, from Local Authorities, Funders, Volunteer Managers, the Voluntary Action History Society and more could join us. Putting together a truly UK-wide team, reaching into many sectors took dedication and more time than we had thought, but to audible sighs of relief, all around, we submitted our proposal to UKRI, Monday 11 June 2020, 11:40. The chair of the Advisory Panel sent this comforting message:

> Many congratulations for achieving this major milestone at such pace, under these highly unusual circumstances. At this early stage of the pandemic, as we learn to live with restrictions, long term health impacts and significant economic damage, our sector will be more important than ever. (Baroness Scott of Needham Market)

Despite her wise prediction, speaking of the early stage of the pandemic, this was the moment of our greatest error. We thought that her comment referred to the early days when we were writing the bid in April and that the pandemic was now largely behind us. We thought that if we were to receive this grant, we would look at events largely retrospectively and that we could inform recovery. We were very wrong.

We learned that the funding proposal had been successful on 30 September 2020. It is testimony to the hard work of colleagues within the various universities involved, that we could start the project officially a month later, 28 October 2020. For those less familiar with academic grant making it must be stressed that seven months between a first email and formally beginning a large project involving six universities, four voluntary sector organisations as co-applicants and two project partner organisations is a remarkably short time and required the goodwill and extra effort of many. We will explain the various components of the project in the chapters of the book. But if you look at the start date of the project you will realise that this was the time when we began to appreciate that the pandemic was not over and that we understood the possibility of future lockdowns. Throughout every period of this project we had to remain agile, responding to an ever-changing environment. That, too, was only possible because of the commitment of many to help us learn and maybe take something positive from this difficult time. Stress was a real ever-present difficulty and everyone involved was affected, be it by becoming ill themselves, home educating or, in the worst cases, experiencing loss and bereavement. Bringing this book to you is only possible, not just through hard work, we are used to that, but through personal endurance and fortitude. Generously caring for each other became part of how we worked together. This book is not just a description of findings from a research project. The way this project was conceived, designed and undertaken reflects a period of all our lives. In that respect this book is a historical record, as an observation of our collective experience. We all, not just the authors, share a common bond in what we felt and experienced during the COVID-19 pandemic. This project took us in anticipated and unanticipated directions, highlighting points of concurrence and departure between the four jurisdictions of the United Kingdom, but also highlighting similarities and differences within and across the research teams, in terms of academic disciplines, ongoing research interests and the different national contexts. It soon transpired that the reason there is not more cross UK devolved assemblies research is that it is immensely complex and difficult, but as this project demonstrated, potentially also highly rewarding.

One finding this book offers in addition, though, is clarity that research and policy in the future must be mindful of the divergence in the nations of the UK. The evidence presented in this book is a clear reminder that research about the UK needs to enquire systematically how a situation is experienced in all its nations, England, Scotland, Wales and Northern Ireland. This book can show you how that is done, with determination and time.

ONE

Researching in a pandemic

Laura Crawford, Irene Hardill and Jurgen Grotz

Image 1.1: 'The Arches' project delivered by Rhayader and District Community Support in Powys, 2020

Note: This community support project recruited additional volunteers to help with prescriptions, shopping, food bank parcels, telephone support, dog walking and delivering a local bulletin

1.1 Spring 2020: COVID-19

This book focuses on the ways in which the COVID-19 pandemic has transformed the landscape of 'voluntary action', that is, the work of voluntary organisations, volunteers and activists (Davis Smith, 2019, p 3) across the four nations of the United Kingdom of Great Britain and Northern Ireland (UK). In March 2020, as a response to the global public health emergency, UK citizens were instructed by the leaders of their respective jurisdictions to stay at home. The declaration of a national emergency was of a magnitude not seen since the Second World War (Calvert and Arbuthnott, 2021). Over a two-year period, unprecedented restrictions to everyday life were imposed by the devolved administrations for Northern Ireland, Scotland, Wales and Westminster for England as health policy is non-reserved, that is, it is devolved and, therefore, not the responsibility of UK government (Hennessy, 2022).

These restrictions placed constraints on volunteer involving organisations (VIOs) delivering their services. As has been reported elsewhere (Ellis Paine, 2020; Macmillan, 2020a; British Academy, 2021; Dayson et al, 2021) especially during the lockdown periods some volunteering projects were paused, such as charity shops and luncheon clubs, while other services, such as befriending, were delivered in different ways, moving from face-to-face to online or by telephone. While the pandemic moved many people to volunteer for the first time (Ellis Paine, 2020), other volunteers were forced to stop because they were instructed to 'shield'. Shielding guidance was introduced in order to protect those who, if exposed to COVID-19, were at the highest risk of severe illness. Those shielding were advised not to leave the house for shopping, leisure or any social gatherings and to minimise any contact. At the same time new mutual aid schemes were established, with many supporting those shielding at home, and new social welfare needs emerged, some on an alarming scale.

In addition to health policy being devolved for decades, voluntary action policy-making is also 'non-reserved' (Woolvin and Hardill, 2013; Woolvin et al, 2015), and this has resulted in variations in relations between the state and voluntary action (Woolvin et al, 2015). The pandemic has brought into sharper focus the realities of policy divergence on the role, position and contribution of voluntary action across the four UK jurisdictions. The impact of the emergence of different relationships between voluntary action and the state across the four nations provides both the context and the framework for analysing the role of voluntary action in the pandemic and beyond in this book.

In 2020, the voluntary and community sector and the social science research community quickly mobilised to collaborate, share and disseminate knowledge on the impact of the pandemic on the sector. The UK Voluntary Sector Studies Network (VSSN), for example, quickly established a repository of relevant pandemic-related research (VSSN, 2020a), and its annual conference in 2020 was held online and was dedicated to the topic (VSSN, 2020b). The editors of *Voluntary Sector Review* launched a call for COVID-19 research notes, which began to be published in 2021 following peer review. In the first lockdown in spring 2020 the authors of this book collaborated to co-design a research project to 'critically evaluate social welfare voluntary action responses to the pandemic, to help guide the UK volunteer effort to support the national recovery and preparedness for future crises'. Funding was sought from the UK Economic and Social Research Council (ESRC) as part of the UK Research and Innovation (UKRI) COVID-19 call. In 2020, UKRI received funds from UK government to support research to inform recovery from the pandemic, specifically new research or innovation with a clear impact pathway that had the potential, within the period of the grant, to deliver a significant contribution to the understanding of, and response to, the impacts of the COVID-19 pandemic (UKRI, 2020). As part of this call ESRC funded short- to medium-term economic and social research activity aimed at addressing and mitigating the health, social, economic and environmental impacts of the pandemic. There was a particular focus on the national response to the pandemic, although some projects were cross-national (ESRC, 2021a). Almost 200 social science projects were funded (ESRC, 2021b), and the project this book draws on represents part of this national research effort.

This introductory chapter briefly introduces the scope of the research underpinning this book and offers definitions of key terms, before explaining the structure of the book.

1.2 The United Kingdom, devolution and public policy

There is a long history to policy and legal divergence between the UK nations and of calls for home rule/devolution (Hardill et al, 2006). Indeed, the three Celtic nations have previously been described as 'hidden' or stateless nations (Roberts and Baker, 2006, p 27). Since 1997, the devolution project has made an ad hoc arrangement more rational and formal (Benneworth, 2006, p 44). The current arrangement can be traced to the 1992 Labour Manifesto, which had a firm commitment to devolution for the island of Great Britain, to Scotland, Wales and the English regions (Benneworth, 2006, p 47). Scotland and Wales were granted devolution through acts of parliament introduced after the referenda held in 1997 initiated by the New Labour government led by Tony Blair. Northern Ireland's conflicts and divisions have given its governance structures a more complicated character (Hughes and Ketola, 2021, p 9). The Good Friday Arrangement signed in 1998 created the power-sharing Northern Ireland Executive and the elected Northern Ireland Assembly, otherwise known as Stormont, but at times, including the period preceding the pandemic, these institutions have been suspended, with direct rule imposed from Westminster (Hughes and Ketola, 2021, p 27). The devolution 'settlement' has not been static;

indeed, its 'architect', in Wales, Ron Davies, described it as a 'process not an event' (Davies, 1999). The National Assembly for Wales gained more powers over the next 20 years and changed its name to the Welsh Parliament in 2020 to reflect its enhanced powers. In Scotland, the transfer of devolved powers commenced with the Scotland Act 1998 which established the Scottish Parliament and transferred some of the powers previously held at Westminster. However, devolution has not stood still since the opening of the Scottish Parliament in 1999, with the transfer of significant new financial powers in 2012, and income tax and welfare powers in 2016. The Scottish National Party (SNP) won the 2021 Scottish Parliamentary Election with a manifesto commitment to hold a legitimate and constitutional referendum on independence within this parliamentary term, if the COVID-19 crisis is over. George Robertson's claim in the mid-1990s, that devolution 'will kill the SNP stone dead' (Taylor, 2015), appears not to have materialised, with increased support for independence in Scotland and Wales, and for the reunification of Ireland. While these issues, such as the 2014 independence referendum in Scotland, pre-date COVID-19 and may also reflect the fall-out of Brexit, as we discuss in Chapter Seven, the divergent responses to the pandemic, particularly the more cautious responses of the devolved administrations to that of the UK Government in England, has further emphasised the possibilities of doing things differently, as illustrated in Table 1.1.

The pandemic was preceded by significant shifts in social policy over a protracted period, which as a result of devolution arrangements played out differently in the four UK nations. This is reflected in variations in relations between the state and the voluntary and community sector (Woolvin et al, 2015). Prior to 2010, despite variations there was a commitment to partnership working across the four nations. In the decade prior to the pandemic in Wales and Scotland the spirit of partnership working between the state and the sector remained strong (Woolvin et al, 2015). In Northern

Table 1.1: Pandemic timelines across the UK nations

	Phases	England	Northern Ireland	Scotland	Wales
2020	Pre-pandemic	31 January first two cases confirmed in England, 27 February first case in Northern Ireland 11 March global pandemic declared			
	First lockdown	23 March	23 March	24 March	23 March
	First lockdown ends	Phased from 13 May	Phased from 18 May	29 May (Phase 1)	1 June
	2020 Autumn lockdowns (firebreaks)	5 November Second national lockdown	19 October Schools close	29 October Local authority protection measures	8 September Local lockdowns 23 October to 9 November National firebreak
	Lockdowns end	2 December Regional tiers			09 November
2021	2021 winter lockdown	6 January Third national lockdown	27 December	5 January	20 December
	Third lockdown ends	Phased from 8 March	5 March	2 April	13 March
	2021 spring easing	Roadmap out of lockdown	12 April All children return to school	26 April Level 3	13 March to 7 August

Table 1.1: Pandemic timelines across the UK nations (continued)

	Phases	England	Northern Ireland	Scotland	Wales
	2021 opening up	19 July 'Unlocking'	April/May Gradual lifting of restrictions	19 July Level 0	7 August to 26 December Alert level 0
	2021 autumn	14 September Autumn winter plan	November/December Strengthening of restrictions as winter pressures build		
	Omicron	8 December Plan 'B'	8 January Omicron dominant variant	26 December to 24 January Additional restrictions	26 December to 28 January Alert level 2
		27 January Plan 'B' restrictions end			28 January Alert level 0
2022	All restrictions lifted	24 February	15 February	21 March	28 March

Ireland, policy-making and partnership working have been strengthened by the Good Friday Agreement, where all the main parties in the devolved administration have embraced the sector (Hughes and Ketola, 2021). In England, the pandemic came at the end of a decade of disengagement from the sector (Woolvin et al, 2015), which Macmillan (2013) has described as a 'partial decoupling'. The pre-existing relationships between the state and the sector have significantly shaped differences in policy and the practice of voluntary action during the pandemic (Macmillan, 2020b).

Since 2020, the devolved nature of policy responses to the pandemic has resulted in an uneven geography across the four UK jurisdictions. The research that underpins this book needed to acknowledge these variations in emergency legislation, for example, social distancing and lockdowns, to capture the contexts voluntary sector organisations were operating within. Recent reports, however, indicate that the impact of these variations in emergency legislation on infections may be less than anticipated (Smith and Menzies, 2022).

1.3 Scope and definitions

The research this book draws on was undertaken in England, Wales, Scotland and Northern Ireland, over a 15-month period, October 2020 to January 2022. The aforementioned ESRC COVID-19 Scheme provided an environment for supporting collaborative partnerships by offering financial support for co-applicants from beyond higher education. The ESRC recognised that some pandemic research would benefit from partnership working as multiple knowledges needed to be mobilised; not merely epistemic knowledge, but also techne and phronesis, the knowledge of practitioners and citizens (Flyvbjerg, 2001). Such knowledge mobilisation is underpinned by collaboration and trust (Flyvbjerg, 2001; Bannister and Hardill, 2014), in our case with experts from the voluntary sector organisations.

As the Scheme stipulated that project findings should inform recovery, we had to plan research that could generate immediate impact within the currency of the award. To this end, we assembled a team including academics spanning human geography, sociology and social policy, and practitioner experts from voluntary sector organisations to co-design the research proposal, in our case four key sector infrastructure bodies for each nation. This was a critical component of our strategy ensuring the voices of those coordinating voluntary action during the pandemic shaped the project from the very outset. We also indicated that we would be supported by a Project Partner Advisory Panel, with representatives from key professional networks, organisations and related ESRC and British Academy investments, to offer critical feedback at key points during the research project. The Advisory Panel enriched our research with insights from different geographical and operational perspectives, with varying degrees of proximity to high-level policy-making and responses on the ground. We also named a number of consultants, including two volunteer involvement digital platform operators, Be Collective and Team Kinetic. These consultants provided data that enabled us to measure how volunteering patterns had changed over the course of the pandemic. An interdisciplinary approach was employed, with a combination of theoretical perspectives, to gather unique pan-UK data from the analysis of four distinctive and divergent national policy contexts that shaped responses to the pandemic.

The spirit of collaboration and co-production that characterised the early stages of research design was sustained throughout project delivery. While co-production has various interpretations (Glynos and Speed, 2012), in the project we conceived it as a process that recognises and foregrounds multiple knowledges (Flyvbjerg, 2001; Hodgkinson et al, 2001). The project team was geographically dispersed across the UK, and each individual brought situated and embodied knowledge (Bondi, 2014) through the lived experience of operating within a specific policy regime, contributing a more nuanced understanding of the realities of policy implementation. The team worked largely in English, but in Wales the bilingual team worked in both Welsh and English: participants may have valued the opportunity to contribute in Welsh. Additionally, through their organisational networks, team members were able to incorporate the perspectives of a diverse range of VIOs.

Defining voluntary action is complex, and never more so than in a period of such transformational change as the pandemic. Like other scholars (Brewis et al, 2021) we used the term 'voluntary action' as a catch-all to encompass the work of voluntary organisations, volunteers and activists (Davis Smith, 2019, p 3). The definition of 'voluntary action' we operationalised was co-produced by the research team and the Advisory Panel, and is broadly based on the definitions of volunteering used by Kearney (2001) and in the Northern Ireland Volunteering Strategy (Department for Social Development, 2012).

> Voluntary Action is the commitment of time and energy, for the benefit of society and the community, the environment or individuals outside (or in addition) to one's immediate family. It is undertaken freely and by choice, without concern for financial gain. It comprises the widest spectrum of activity for example, community development, arts, sport, faith based, education, neighbourliness, youth, environmental, health and direct care. This can include activities undertaken through public, private and voluntary organisations as well as community participation and social action in associations and groups which may not be registered or don't have a confirmed structure. (Grotz, 2021, p 9)

There is no universal term used across the four UK nations to describe the sector, and a range of different terms are explained in the Glossary. The sector remains a 'loose and baggy monster' to coin the phrase used by Kendall and Knapp (1995). In each national chapter the appropriate terminology is used, so variations in terminology will feature across the book. Moreover, the authorship of the national chapters represents the diverse voices and perspectives of our pan-UK team. In other chapters, the term voluntary sector is used to refer to the collective work of voluntary organisations or VIOs. Other terms which appear in the book are the voluntary and community sector and the 'third sector', which is now seen as inextricably linked to the New Labour years in England, and 'civil society' which came to be the preferred term of the Westminster Conservative and Coalition governments of the 2010s. Some other terms that need to be explained, especially for non-Scottish readers include: Third Sector Interfaces (TSIs) which provide a single point of access for support and advice for the third sector within each of Scotland's 32 local authority areas. Infrastructure organisations support and/or coordinate volunteering across an area or sector and include local organisations such as TSIs and local authorities; and national organisations such as Volunteer Scotland and the Scottish Council for Voluntary Organisations, and sectoral umbrella bodies. For non-Welsh readers, County Voluntary Councils (CVCs) are local umbrella infrastructure organisations. These broadly operate on the basis of local authority areas in Wales, with 19 CVCs covering the 22 local authority areas: the Gwent Association of Voluntary Organisation operates across Blaenau Gwent, Caerphilly, Monmouthshire and Newport. The CVCs provide established dialogue routes to health boards, Welsh Government, local authorities and other boards.

1.4 Researching voluntary action: approach and methods

To achieve the aims of our empirical study, three key research questions were examined: first, in what ways do the voluntary action policy frameworks adopted by the four nations in response to COVID-19 differ? And how effective were they?

Second, who responded to the call to volunteer during the COVID-19 pandemic? Did the profile of volunteers change? How can we sustain the involvement of new volunteers beyond the pandemic? Third, are there examples of good practice for voluntary action to support communities and individuals in times of crisis? In what ways can good practice be shared? And are they transferable across the jurisdictions?

The team collaborated to prepare the research funding application in spring 2020, during the first lockdown, when we were all unable to leave home. Consequently, we planned remote data collection methods involving our practitioner experts', research team's and Advisory Panel's organisational networks as amplifiers and gatekeepers to reach a range of VIOs and policy-makers.

The ESRC COVID-19 Scheme provided the resources to fund the time and intellectual space needed to meaningfully co-produce research and to plan a participative project with some latitude to allow for adjustments to data collection and anticipated outcomes in an emergency. We were, therefore, able to undertake 'transformative', as opposed to 'additive', co-production, an opportunity to make real and meaningful change for all parties involved (Glynos and Speed, 2012). Once we began the project, the practice of co-producing knowledge had to be negotiated and then activated (Bannister and Hardill, 2014). It was transformative in the sense that the research was designed to gather the evidence the sector needed to understand the impact of the pandemic, thereby enabling us to understand a specific historical moment through the application of a process of developing a Theory of Change.

Theory of Change approaches were introduced in international development to assess programme effectiveness, in particular to understand how and why a desired change might happen (Weiss, 1972). They have now been widely adapted to support programme design and evaluation in work to understand complex systems, for example, in Rapid Evidence Assessments (Stuart et al, 2020). Our team worked in different spatial and policy contexts, making it imperative that we found a mutually agreeable set of terms to describe the key objects of study. To assist this process a modified virtual Delphi exercise was facilitated. Our Delphi exercise included iterative communications of the emerging Theory of Change, initially to the research team and subsequently to the Advisory Panel, which were systematically analysed, to gain a shared understanding of the research questions and a common approach to data gathering and analysis.

The research adopted an interdisciplinary approach, which entailed integrating knowledge and methods from different disciplines, and synthesising approaches to link the four UK nations. A mixed-methods approach was employed to focus on the policy and organisational responses to coordinating and managing volunteers during the pandemic across the four nations. The methodology involved four key work packages that were designed to gather a range of data sources at speed and included: analysis of policy documents and published research; a call for evidence, which later became four national surveys; elite interviews; and an analysis of digital volunteer matching services' data. The team assembled in different configurations to support the delivery of these work packages, sometimes working in national teams to gather perspectives from one specific policy context and, in other cases, working across the UK to draw broader conclusions about some of the cross-cutting challenges facing the sector. The central UK team helped coordinate activity and draw together the different dimensions of the project, and lead on the integrated analysis.

The analysis of key policy documents was conducted in two stages, first, each national team identified a landmark policy document that pre-dated the pandemic and set the tone for volunteering policy within that jurisdiction. Between-case discourse analysis revealed variations in the framing of voluntary action across the UK. The second stage involved a within-case analysis, to explore policy-making during the pandemic, specifically within the time period between

23 March 2020 and 22 March 2021, from the start of the first emergency to the easing of restrictions in spring 2021. The analysis was conducted by a member of the central UK team who had 'distance' from the lived realities of coordinating voluntary action during the pandemic. As a result, this component of the analysis was driven by policy discourses, although feedback was provided by voluntary sector team members in each jurisdiction.

The team worked in close partnership with two volunteer management app providers. Be Collective and Team Kinetics' platforms provided organisations with the technological tools to digitally recruit volunteers and promote volunteering opportunities. The providers extracted anonymised demographic and deployment data to offer a snapshot into volunteering patterns for the period March 2019 to August 2021. Initial scoping meetings helped establish what data were available and the format in which it could be shared. These datasets were cleaned before running statistical analyses on key trends (see Chapter Two). The dataset supplemented our emerging knowledge base by observing the ebbs and flows in voluntary activity over the course of the pandemic and included demographic data about the volunteer cohort.

When we wrote the research proposal in spring 2020 we anticipated undertaking a call for evidence to capture voluntary sector experiences of the pandemic, but by the time we started the project in autumn 2020 this needed to be reimagined because so much material was already published (see Chapter Two). By October 2020, the voluntary sector and research community had already begun to examine some of the successes and challenges of the initial response to the pandemic, especially focusing on the first lockdown of spring 2020. Additionally, team members reported a widespread sense of survey fatigue across the sector, with organisations that were already stretched beyond capacity being repeatedly asked to contribute to research studies. There was a general reluctance to circulate yet another survey in autumn 2020, so it was essential that we adopted a dynamic approach to our methodology in response to these concerns and to situate our study within this emerging discourse. Our call for evidence became a two-stage process, first, we called for our team to gather relevant evidence from published material in each of their jurisdictions. After these documents were compiled, we systematically reviewed the existing published material before creating four national surveys that would be designed to explicitly respond to gaps in this corpus of knowledge. A thematic analysis of over 70 published reports was subsequently conducted to supplement our existing work packages; to identify what was already known; and to reaffirm where our study was poised to respond to gaps in knowledge (Crawford, 2021). The key themes that arose from this analysis are discussed in Chapter Two.

The outcomes of this analysis were actively embedded into our evolving research design, with the analysis of existing material presented to the core group, and members of the Advisory Panel for feedback and to determine to what extent the themes resonated. Through these discussions, a list of core questions was agreed. These were questions that would feature in some form in each national survey and they related to topics aligned with our overarching research questions, and where there were gaps in existing knowledge. Each national team then decided what additional questions to add and in what format some of the core questions would be posed. These decisions were driven by a need to generate data that could influence and contribute to an emerging discourse within each jurisdiction. For example, in Wales, the additional questions were guided by the publication of the Welsh Parliament Equality, Local Government and Communities Committee's February 2021 report on the impact of COVID-19 on the voluntary sector. Questions were shaped by the report's recommendations, including a specific focus on social value. In Scotland and Northern Ireland there was a greater use of numerical measures to quantify the major issues impacting organisations.

In addition, each national team adopted a bespoke sampling strategy. For example, in England the survey was circulated as an open call for local authorities, infrastructure organisations and VIOs across the voluntary, public and private sectors. In Northern Ireland the survey was sent to nominated individuals within regional infrastructure organisations, local government and Health and Social Care Trusts. The surveys were also circulated at slightly different times in spring/summer 2021, with the dates carefully selected to maximise response rates, and fit within the existing calendar of activity of our partner organisations. The findings from the survey will be discussed in the subsequent national chapters.

From a methodological standpoint, this engagement with existing research boosted the credibility of our research. By clearly signalling how our study was different and enhanced existing knowledge, there was a hope that organisations would deem the findings valuable. The thematic analysis formed the basis of many of the presentations delivered at online workshops and mid-project briefing events during the currency of the project. In these fora, we disseminated our analysis of some of the themes consistently reported across the published research. Workshops and briefing events served a dual purpose as both a forum for sharing emerging findings but also as a chance to incorporate new insights into our ongoing research, particularly around how certain types of organisation experienced certain challenges more acutely than others. These conversations were particularly fruitful in sense checking our assessment of some of the challenges facing the sector with organisations operating at different spatial scales working with different demographic groups. Moreover, we were able to provide overviews of our analysis of the broader research context which provided an opportunity for organisations to reflect on how their experiences resonated with the existing evidence.

The online surveys were circulated in spring/early summer of 2021. The timings of the surveys enabled us to capture key moments in the pandemic, moving beyond the initial response to consider the challenges of mobilising voluntary action through the partial easing of restrictions in summer 2020 to the subsequent winter lockdowns of late 2020 to early 2021. The survey investigated the evolving nature of societal need through the fluctuations of infection levels and restrictions. We sought to gauge the multifaceted ways the sector was supporting communities after the initial emergency response, especially surrounding some of the more deeply entrenched inequalities exposed and exacerbated by the pandemic. Ultimately, the surveys provided an opportunity to enhance knowledge by viewing the pandemic not as one singular event, but rather of several emergencies, and as a constantly evolving landscape that placed different pressures on how the voluntary sector operated and the availability of volunteers.

The elite interviews with policy-makers and sector experts were conducted towards the latter part of the project. By this stage our national teams had gathered survey data from a broad range of organisations operating at different spatial scales and responding to different societal needs. Each national team identified five interviewees due to their proximity to policy-making/influencing, including representatives from large VIOs and local authorities. The interviews added additional depth to the survey data and provided rich insights into what happened during the pandemic, the impact of policy and the future implications for the sector.

While this 15-month research project could capture relevant information from before and during the beginning of the pandemic, unexpectedly, it was not able to capture its end. Furthermore, the national restrictions varied during the time the project was undertaken.

1.5 About this book

The structure of the book is representative of the collaborative research approach adopted. Following this introductory chapter, Chapter Two describes the data collection activities that were conducted at the UK level including the discourse analysis of pandemic policy documents, a thematic analysis of research on the impact of the pandemic on voluntary action published in 2020 and an analysis of volunteer management app data from Team Kinetic and Be Collective. Chapter Two also charts the policy divergence across the devolved administrations before moving to consider some of the overarching demographic trends captured in the app data and points of similarity in the response within communities.

The following four chapters explore the mobilisation of voluntary action as a response to the pandemic in the four respective national contexts. Each chapter follows the same basic structure and is co-authored by the national teams. The same methods were employed across the four countries, and these chapters begin with an analysis of the sector in 2020, then focus on the pandemic, and then look forward drawing on policy documents, published research on the impact of the pandemic on voluntary action, our national surveys and elite interviews. The final chapter draws together the findings across the four nations and summarises the key messages of the book, including a reflection on the legacy of the pandemic on voluntary action.

TWO

Voluntary action and the pandemic across the UK

Ewen Speed, Laura Crawford and Alasdair Rutherford

Image 2.1: Volunteer Bikers NI delivering prescriptions in Northern Ireland

2.1 Introduction

This chapter will explore the implications of the pandemic in terms of constructing respective voluntary action policies across the four UK jurisdictions, particularly in relation to identifying both similarities and differences across the four jurisdictions. It will do this in three primary ways. First, by identifying and analysing policy documents within each of the four jurisdictions, we establish the prevailing policy contexts and how these impacted upon the respective government responses to the pandemic. Second, we consider the impact of the pandemic on the dynamics of voluntary action for the UK population, and what this might tell us about the general impact of the pandemic on public engagement with voluntary action. Third, we present a thematic analysis of a substantial corpus of reports detailing how a diverse range of organisations were engaging with the pandemic conditions. This review identifies some key themes relevant to the voluntary action response including the role of mutual aid and hyper-local activity, the importance of collaboration, partnership and innovation, and how the perceived nature of societal need influenced volunteering trends. The chapter offers a range of analysis across civil society, allowing us a snapshot of the pandemic relations between government, volunteer involving organisations and individual citizens. It also considers evidence of what organisations think is significant in terms of their ongoing response to COVID-19, such as the need to offer more flexible volunteering opportunities and concerns around the inclusion of more diverse groups of people undertaking voluntary action.

2.1.1 Consideration of similarities and differences

The public health response in the UK to the COVID-19 pandemic can be understood as a natural experiment. Citizens of the different jurisdictions were randomly assigned, through their geographical location, to different public health response categories. There was clear divergence across the different jurisdictions. For example, policies were implemented around mandated mask-wearing at different dates across the UK, despite relatively similar rates of infection. At the point of the initial outbreak in March 2020, faced with much ignorance about what the best public health responses might be, the four jurisdictions clearly responded differently to the developing crisis. For this chapter, this could be understood in terms of what the presented evidence can tell us about what the perceived, most proportionate public health response was, in the context of the extant voluntary action context that was in place in each of the four jurisdictions. In turn, this functions to offer crucial insights into the similarities and differences in voluntary action between the jurisdictions and what this might tell us about pandemic responses.

In this regard, the differences in the public health responses to the pandemic across the four jurisdictions presented a novel window into the devolved politics in the UK. This was largely because both public health and voluntary action are areas of unreserved devolved policy-making. This means they are entirely determined at a devolved level, by the respective assembly or parliament. In turn, this creates an opportunity for divergence in terms of policy-making. For example, there were clear similarities in terms of national lockdowns in each jurisdiction, as well as legislation around social distancing and such-like, but there were also differences in the public health response such as in the timing and scope of national lockdowns. This chapter explores these similarities and differences across the four jurisdictions and considers what this might tell us about ongoing voluntary action in a devolved United Kingdom.

2.2 Governing voluntary action in a pandemic: the policy response

The analysis detailed in this section considered a range of voluntary action policy documents from across the four jurisdictions that were published between 23 March 2020 and

22 March 2021. This timeframe marks the 12-month period from the initial UK-wide COVID-19 lockdown. Other inclusion criteria were that the documents, press releases, official policy documents or reports had to be issued by the respective jurisdictional government, at a national level, with one notable exception, the 2020 Kruger Review. More detailed analysis of the underlying voluntary action policy differences across the UK jurisdictions is offered in Speed (2021). Similarly, more detailed analysis of the differences in terms of voluntary action and COVID-19 response are offered in Speed (2022). The analysis of the different jurisdictions that follows is presented alphabetically, commencing with England.

2.2.1 The English case

The review of outputs for England identified six documents that were in scope. These were four documents published by the UK Government, but only relevant to the English context (see UK Government, 2020a, 2020b, 2020c, 2020d) and a further two documents produced by NHS England (see NHS England, 2020a, 2020b). The final English document was a report for government compiled by a member of the UK Parliament into effective community responses to the pandemic. It is this document which the analysis considers first.

The report titled 'Levelling up our communities: Proposals for a new social covenant', the so-called Kruger Review (Kruger, 2020), has commanded a high-profile role in discussions about the English government's response to COVID-19. It is not a clear and direct policy action from government, but it is the closest that the English case came to issuing a national policy. It needs to be noted that there were explicitly labelled policy documents and strategy documents, but these tended to be published by the Local Government Association (LGA) at a local level (for example, LGA, 2020). The Kruger Review engaged with these issues at a national level, from a central 'English' government perspective, thereby meriting consideration here. This differentiation between local and national policy contexts reflects the extent to which the underlying English voluntary action policy framework determined the types of English voluntary action organisational response, that is, the English policy response tended to be dissipated down to a number of different local responses, without recourse to a broader national strategy.

The English policy context is one where voluntary action, and the organisations involved in coordinating voluntary action, are actively seen to be separate from government. The role of government in this sphere is to ensure citizens have the opportunity to participate in voluntary action, but in this regard, government is an enabler rather than a provider of these opportunities. The organisations that actually provide these opportunities are seen as being outside of and apart from government. This was reflected in the focus of the remaining documents which were oriented towards the provision of public health guidelines intended to facilitate ongoing voluntary action in face of the pandemic.

Since the 'Big Society' policy agenda in 2010, the English policy context has tended to see voluntary action as a domain which was not the responsibility of government. This is evidenced directly in the publication of the 2018 'Civil society strategy: Building a future that works for everyone' (Cabinet Office, 2018), in which emphasis is placed on government as an enabler of civil society actors, working in collaboration with private sector actors. In terms of the specific policy response to COVID-19, the primary national level response was concerned with public health guidance. The prevailing policy context, from 2018, mitigated against the development of any concerted national governmental level of English voluntary action policy. Voluntary action policy is diffuse, atomised and highly localised, such that the idea of a national level voluntary action policy becomes hard to imagine. These more local modes of organisation contribute to a set of conditions which facilitate the political choice not to prioritise voluntary action at the national level. The refusal of government to organise a national policy level response meant that much of the policy context was national public health guidelines.

2.2.2 The Northern Irish case

The policy context in Northern Ireland in relation to the devolved assembly is somewhat different to the situation in any of the other jurisdictions. In effect there was no devolved government in Northern Ireland between March 2017 and January 2020. This was due to political cross-party difficulties in forming an Executive. The net effect of this was that many Northern Irish policy decisions were made by the UK Government during this time. This functioned to create something of a policy vacuum in Northern Ireland. However, the Northern Irish policy analysis identified five documents that were within scope. Three of these were issued by the Department for Communities (2020a, 2020b, 2020c) a further one by the Department of Education (2020) and one from the Office of Northern Ireland Direct Government Services (2020).

Four of the documents identified were guidance documents, aimed at outlining best practice for becoming or continuing to engage in voluntary action. In this sense, they were similar to the English case. The fifth document, 'Volunteering during the Coronavirus (COVID-19) pandemic' (Office of Northern Ireland Direct Government Services, 2020) was different in that it took a strategic, more policy-oriented approach. It proposed a national response to the pandemic and was allied to a programme of work, albeit an un-costed programme of work. The emphasis across the document was very much on cross-community collaboration and coordination of activities. The policy documents spoke to a clearly defined voluntary action sector operating at a national level within Northern Ireland, and it is this sector, coupled to local community groupings, which the voluntary action policies sought to engage and work with. The lack of a more explicit and sustained voluntary action policy programme in Northern Ireland may be more indicative of the ongoing difficulties associated with maintaining a fully functioning legislature rather than any wider comment about the state of voluntary action policy in Northern Ireland.

2.2.3 The Scottish case

The documentary analysis identified four documents that were in scope. All four were published by the Scottish Government (2020a, 2020b, 2020c, 2020d) and none of them were guidance documents contra to what was identified in the preceding analyses of England and Northern Ireland. The Scotland COVID-19 policy response was more directive and programmatic than the other jurisdictions. For example, among a wide range of support made available across the third and private sectors, the Scottish Government provided a £350 million package of support to be invested in communities, such as the 'Supporting Communities Fund'.

Within the 2020–1 Programme for Government there was a commitment to ensure that the third sector and volunteering can 'thrive and contribute to a recovering economy and society' (Scottish Government, 2020b, p 60). Across the policy documents reviewed there was little direct and explicit voluntary action policy identified. However, it was very apparent that the third sector was centrally and directly invoked into the job of partnership and collaboration with the Scottish Government. This is a fundamental difference from the English and Northern Irish analysis in that voluntary action was construed as a direct responsibility of national level government, however, this is disbursed to local levels. The Scottish case is marked by a national policy level commitment to collaboration and partnership between voluntary action organisations and government, much more so than the English or Northern Irish contexts.

2.2.4 The Welsh case

The document search identified four documents which were in scope. Three of these were published by the Government of Wales (2020a, 2020b, 2020c) and the fourth was a report from an official inquiry conducted by the Welsh Senedd into the initial Welsh Government response to COVID-19 (Welsh Parliament Equality, Local Government, and Communities Committee, 2021). In terms of voluntary action and COVID-19, the response was coordinated by Wales Council for Voluntary Action (WCVA), a national membership body for voluntary action in Wales. The WCVA is not a government body so does not have the authority to make national policy. There were many policy documents produced by the WCVA but they were not included for analysis here.

Of the four identified documents the most analytically interesting was the initial guidance on support for the third sector which was published within the first week of the UK-wide lockdown. This document announced £24 million of additional funding across three broad strands of activity: first, the Third Sector Resilience Fund, helping charities and third sector organisations through the crisis; second, by helping more people volunteer; and third, by strengthening the third sector infrastructure. This response demonstrated a clear national commitment to increasing levels of voluntary action at national and local levels. The national disbursement of the Third Sector Resilience Fund was to be coordinated by WCVA. This indicates a real commitment to collaborative partnership across government and voluntary action organisations and, in stark contrast to the English case, demonstrates engagement, on the part of national government, with existing structures within the voluntary action sphere.

The analyses presented here demonstrate the ways in which the prevailing policy contexts differed across the four UK jurisdictions. The implications of these differences become clear when we consider how the prevailing policy contexts both structure and are structured by the policy responses in relation to voluntary action and COVID-19. It could be argued that the English case is best characterised by a lack of national policy response. This is largely because responsibility for voluntary action has been rescinded by national government and pushed down to a more local level. In relation to Northern Ireland, the lack of a functioning legislature has impacted on the policy context in myriad ways and the Northern Irish response tended more towards a reliance on public health guidance rather than voluntary action strategic policy, although there was a national level policy response. In contrast, the policy responses in Scotland and Wales have demonstrated consistent national level responses. Typically, these responses have involved collaboration and partnership between voluntary action organisations and national level government. These differences raise important questions about their impact upon the overlap between policy and practice across the four jurisdictions. However, it is also necessary for us to understand the impact of the pandemic on voluntary action at a general level, such that local and national policies might be developed to respond to that context. It is to this issue that we now turn.

2.3 Describing the dynamics of volunteering during the pandemic: the citizen response

Volunteering during the pandemic ebbed and flowed as restrictions were tightened and then relaxed. The available evidence suggests a mixed impact, with formal volunteering, undertaken in the context of an organisation, affected somewhat differently from informal volunteering, activity taken outside of an organisation. Evidence from the Community Life Survey (Department for Digital, Culture, Media and Sport, 2021) shows that formal volunteering rates in England fell sharply in 2020/1 from 37 per cent to 30 per cent of the population, while informal volunteering held steady. Regular, monthly, formal volunteering also fell during the pandemic, while regular informal volunteering rose substantially from 28 per cent to 47 per cent. There was a similar picture in Scotland, where formal volunteering held steady at 26 per cent in 2020, most likely due to the significant growth in mutual aid volunteering which counteracted the decline in formal volunteering. In contrast, informal volunteering increased very significantly from 36 per cent to 56 per cent (Scottish Government, 2022c).

While these large surveys produce a representative snapshot of volunteering at discrete points during the period, it is important to understand how the dynamics of volunteering interacted with pandemic restrictions. Administrative data from digital volunteer-matching services provides us with real-time data on the number of people coming forward to participate in a formal volunteering capacity, and can help us to understand how different groups' opportunities to volunteer were affected by the restrictions. While the data does not cover all volunteers, and there are many routes to volunteering, the scale and real-time nature of the digital data do provide insights not easily achievable with other methods. Significant numbers of individuals responded to the start of the crisis by registering to volunteer. However, the challenges facing organisations in responding to the crisis meant that it was not possible to mobilise the large numbers of people volunteering. In the second lockdown there was a further surge in voluntary action, and this time organisations were in a better position to match people to volunteering roles.

Technology made registering to volunteer easier than it otherwise would have been during the pandemic. While the profile of volunteer registrants tends to be younger than volunteers more broadly, the digital-matching services were used by quite broad demographics in terms of age, gender, rurality and deprivation, with strong patterns showing that they were being accessed by 'different' people than had been using them pre-pandemic as a way to volunteer. This might suggest a very real public response to the perceived pandemic crisis.

2.3.1 Thousands of people responded to lockdown by volunteering

Patterns of formal volunteering engagement were broadly similar across nations, but with differences across time. All four nations showed large spikes in the number of people coming forward to volunteer in late March and April 2020. Figure 2.1 shows the number of volunteer registrations recorded in the data in each of the four nations over time. What is striking is the similarity across the nations in both the patterns and timing.

This response was both rapid and unprecedented in scale. However, organisations faced significant challenges in matching volunteers, as COVID-19 restrictions prevented some volunteer activities and organisations from navigating the fast-changing regulations. From the wider project we know that organisations had significant challenges in mobilising such a large number of volunteers in a short space of time, particularly when also navigating COVID-19 restrictions, such as requirements for shielding and social distancing, as well as the ongoing pandemic pressures themselves (Rutherford and Spath, 2021). Due to this, the number of volunteering opportunities available dropped off steeply as the volunteer numbers increased. This means that large numbers of people were not matched to a volunteering activity.

It is impossible to tell from our data whether this significant number of people went on to volunteer in other ways, either through other formal routes or through informal volunteering and other community action. But it is clear that it was simply not possible to manage the sheer scale of the voluntary action response to the crisis of the pandemic, and this was the case across all four nations.

In contrast, the second, smaller surge in voluntary action associated with the winter lockdowns in 2020 and early 2021 tells a different story. Again, we saw large numbers of new volunteers registering. But this time match rates to activity went up rather than down, and the time between registration and activity fell rather than rose. While in part determined

Figure 2.1: Number of volunteer registrations

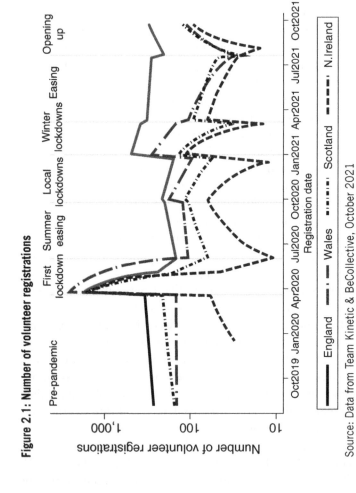

Source: Data from Team Kinetic & BeCollective, October 2021

by the variation in lockdown restrictions, this likely reflects volunteer involving organisations' greater readiness, both in terms of the policies and procedures in place, to provide COVID-safe volunteering, and the anticipation of greater supply that allowed the opportunities for volunteers to be in place. Also, perhaps it was no longer a novel situation and people had better knowledge about what to expect and what would be required. This time the numbers of voluntary action opportunities were increasing again, and there was more clarity about how volunteering could be undertaken within pandemic restrictions. This might reflect the utility of the public health policy guidelines detailed in section 2.2. This meant that a much greater proportion of volunteers were successfully matched to opportunities.

It would be unreasonable to expect that organisations would be able to respond as quickly in a fast-developing and unprecedented crisis such as the first lockdown. However, the second lockdown response shows that with the right policies and preparation in place organisations can mobilise to cope with a dramatic surge in the supply of volunteers.

2.3.2 A different profile of volunteer

COVID-19 has accelerated many aspects of digital society, particularly in relation to public service provision (Peek et al, 2020). The volunteers who came forward through the digital volunteer-matching services at the start of lockdowns differed from the profile of volunteers before the pandemic across all four nations. Lockdown volunteers were older, with those in their 30s, 40s and 50s showing particular growth in participation. This was repeated in the winter lockdown and was likely driven by a combination of furlough and home-working facilitating volunteering. While lockdown volunteering brought in many new people to volunteering, it also risked excluding some groups. Again, it is striking how similar patterns are across the nations. Lockdown volunteers were less likely than those pre-pandemic to come from the most deprived areas, and this is particularly prominent in the second lockdown. In both lockdowns the surge of volunteers were much more likely to have come from rural areas than at other times. These patterns are likely to reflect both differences in the profile of people who were volunteering, as well as a broadening of the demographic using digital routes to volunteer opportunities.

2.3.3 Returning to 'normal'?

By September 2021, the end of our study period, the numbers and characteristics of volunteers had largely returned to the pre-COVID-19 average across the nations. For more detailed characteristics, we must combine data across the nations due to relatively small samples. But this reveals some interesting patterns across time. The average age of new volunteers fell again, as participation among those in their 30s to 50s fell. The number of opportunities has started growing again. However, we are also concerned about the groups for whom volunteering has not returned to normal. Participation among those in the most deprived areas has not bounced back to pre-pandemic levels. It would appear that COVID-19 has exacerbated existing exclusions which are mitigating against a number of groups being able to engage in voluntary action.

For example, Figure 2.2 shows that volunteers reporting disabilities were much less likely to volunteer during both the first and second lockdown. This might reflect the increased COVID-19 risk to some people in this group. The proportion of volunteers with disabilities grew through spring and summer of 2021 as restrictions eased and COVID-19 numbers fell. After the significant relaxation of restrictions in July 2021, and as COVID-19 numbers started to grow again, the numbers of volunteers with disabilities started to fall steeply again (see Figure 2.2). This reflects the complex interplay of COVID-19 restrictions, with existing and developing underlying health risks.

Figure 2.2: Proportion of disabled volunteers

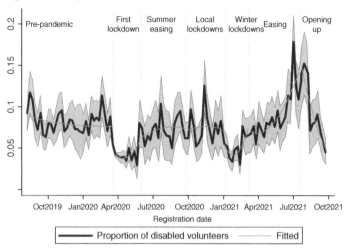

Source: Data from Team Kinetic, October 2021

2.3.4 Understanding volunteering during the pandemic

This analysis also helps us to shed light on the dynamics that may lie behind the patterns in formal volunteering observed in the survey data (Department for Digital, Culture, Media and Sport, 2021). The fall in formal volunteering participation does not seem to have been driven by a fall in the willingness to volunteer, but instead by the effect that restrictions had on whether opportunities were available to volunteer.

Where we need to be cautious is the extent to which we might say that volunteering is returning to 'normal'. Some deviations from normal are to be welcomed: more use of technology to access volunteering; and a broader profile of volunteers using that technology. But others might create cause for concern: the falling participation of those in the more deprived communities; and the decline in volunteer registrations among disabled volunteers.

Conclusions drawn from this analysis, therefore, must only be taken together with the evidence from across these domains. But what is striking is how similar the patterns are across the nations. We see the same spikes in registrations, and the same patterns in activity. Despite different policy responses and timing, the broad pandemic phases do seem to match to changes in the numbers and profile of volunteers over time. And by late 2021, we see most characteristics returning to pre-pandemic levels across the four jurisdictions.

Overall, we can be reassured that volunteering on the whole is resilient. The challenges of the first lockdown did not deter volunteers registering in the second. Where formal volunteering was not possible, informal volunteering seems to have sprung up in its place. On most characteristics, volunteer registrations have returned to normal. But we must be concerned with those who risk being left behind due to COVID-19 risks as society returns to normal if volunteering is to be a diverse and inclusive activity. This may require fresh thinking in the ways in which people can get involved, and feel safe in their involvement, as we come out of the COVID-19 pandemic.

So far, we have considered the policy responses to voluntary action in the context of the pandemic, and the citizen response to voluntary action in the context of the pandemic. Now we consider the role of the voluntary action organisations themselves.

2.4 Coordinating the voluntary action response: the organisational response

In order to assess the organisational response to the pandemic, we undertook qualitative analysis of published research which captured common organisational experiences of responding to the pandemic. Over 70 reports from voluntary and community sector organisations were compiled for analysis. These were wide-reaching in scope and content, and represented a broad range of organisations, including reports produced by individual charities, think tanks and infrastructure organisations. Similar overarching themes were observed surrounding the challenges and successes of coordinating voluntary action in the face of the unfolding pandemic. In spite of these similarities, there was a clear geographical unevenness in the quantity of published material in each jurisdiction.

2.4.1 Key themes in the thematic analysis

A range of methods were employed across these studies including interviews, focus groups, surveys and case studies. While many of the reports referenced the UK, few explicitly discussed experiences in Northern Ireland, further evidencing the need for a UK-wide study. The reports analysed ranged from those published in the immediate aftermath of the first lockdown in March 2020 up to the end of February 2021. The majority of the reports reflected on patterns observed in spring/early summer 2020, with less coverage on the impact of fluctuating infection levels and government restrictions in the late summer/winter months. The focus of the reports also varied considerably, from those exploring how volunteer involving organisations adapted their working practices, to those focusing on the issues the voluntary and public sector were addressing, for example, loneliness and isolation, supporting those who were shielding, to reports that commented on the changing nature of volunteer engagement.

Three central overarching themes which appeared repeatedly across the 70 reports were, first, the importance of mutual aid, second, the value of collaboration and, third, issues around digital technologies, each of which will be discussed in this chapter. In terms of mutual aid, there was widespread recognition that mutual aid and hyper-local groups were instrumental in providing emergency support within place-based communities. As Tiratelli and Kaye (2020, p 28) argue, 'these groups are not a "nice-to-have" – they are of decisive importance to the health and welfare of thousands of people'. Mutual aid offered an agile, flexible and responsive approach to addressing societal need, often mobilising far more quickly than formal organisations, who had to adopt new systems and processes of remote working (Tiratelli and Kaye, 2020; Curtin et al, 2021). In terms of collaboration, relationships and partnerships were cited as critical. There were numerous examples of good collaborative practice where organisations worked together, playing to their strengths to coordinate activity, while in other areas tensions arose in defining who was best placed to respond, often resulting in duplication (Cretu, 2020). The MOVE project analysed data from different local authority areas in England, Scotland and Wales to classify different response models. Three frameworks were identified that captured the ways different stakeholders brokered relationships and collaborated to coordinate voluntary action (Burchell et al, 2020). The strength of pre-existing relationships across sectors and the size of the area played a role in determining how collaborations played out during the pandemic. The issue of collaboration echoes some of the policy analysis in section 2.2, where different jurisdictions were characterised by fundamentally different approaches to the ethos of collaborative working.

In terms of digital technologies, numerous examples of innovative approaches and processes were observed (Cretu, 2020). The pandemic has clearly accelerated the adoption of digital tools to recruit, support and manage voluntary action (Donahue et al, 2020). Some activities that were traditionally carried out face-to-face, for example, befriending, were reimagined as virtual or telephone services. While digital technologies had a transformative impact, facilitating connection at a safe distance, the move to digital exposed inequalities in digital knowledge and access (Welsh Parliament Equality, Local Government, and Communities Committee, 2021). Such findings cautioned against seeing 'digital' as a one-size-fits-all approach to facilitating voluntary action in the wake of COVID-19.

In addition to capturing what was happening on the ground in response to pandemic conditions of voluntary action, reports had already begun to speculate on what recovery might look like, and whether the innovations COVID-19 prompted would have a long-lasting legacy. These reflections were most insightful in determining some of the conditions that either underpinned or acted as barriers to effective voluntary action pandemic responses. The pandemic radically transformed working life, with the furlough scheme and surge in remote working increasing volunteer availability, enabling some who had not volunteered before to take on roles (Coutts et al, 2020). Conversely, pandemic restrictions curtailed the involvement of many long-standing volunteers who were forced to shield or whose roles no longer existed. As Ellis Paine (2020) notes, the pandemic saw individuals both step up and stand down from volunteering, with calls to consider the long-term impact on those who paused their involvement during the pandemic (Grotz et al, 2020). This finding was also evidenced in the analysis presented in section 2.3.

Across the board, funding was a concern, with the flexibility of some responses constrained by funding dedicated to specific projects. Some reports advocated for future funding to target core organisational costs to enable more agile responses (Coutts et al, 2020; Wilson et al, 2020a). While on the surface many comparable patterns were observed in volunteering activity, the pandemic revealed the relative strength of pre-existing relationships and infrastructures (Wilson et al, 2020b; Wyler, 2020). Moreover, the pandemic exposed the legacy of previous investment, particularly given that joined-up responses were reported in areas with social and community-led infrastructure and in areas with previous experience of cross-sector emergency responses, for example, those prone to flooding (Wyler, 2020). This would suggest that those jurisdictions with more facilitative, partnership-based policies were better placed to respond to the pandemic. At a national, UK level, variations in funding and infrastructure did not impact upon the number of citizens volunteering to help, but they do appear to have had an effect on how enthusiasm to volunteer was converted into meaningful action.

2.5 Conclusion

In comparing the four nations, we faced the challenge of disentangling the different COVID-19 responses at governmental, citizen and organisational level. What this analysis demonstrates is that there were marked similarities between the four jurisdictions, and that there were marked differences. As we write this some months after the initial lockdowns in the UK, it is hard to assess whether any of these differences had any significant impact on the progression of the pandemic. For example, volunteering numbers across the four jurisdictions are now broadly similar, as indeed they were throughout the initial responses and subsequent lockdowns. Yet what they do suggest, and indeed even evidence, are fundamental differences, across the devolved assemblies of the UK, to the role and function of voluntary action in relation to the state and voluntary action organisations. The citizen response was largely similar across the respective jurisdictions. However, how well voluntary action organisations were able to deploy these volunteers was impacted by previous experience, and the organisational context in which they were located. If there was a commitment to collaboration and partnership working then this led to more effective organisation of the voluntary action response. In terms of the policy context, both Scotland and Wales, at the level of national government, had a voluntary action policy regime characterised by partnership and participation between voluntary action organisations and government.

The challenges of measuring the impact of policy differences can also be observed in public health policy; rates of COVID-19 transmission and mortality are not significantly different between the four UK jurisdictions in spite of policy differences.

This may reflect the contagious nature of COVID-19, it may reflect economic arguments for opening up winning out globally, against public health arguments for locking down. The fact of the matter is, we are still in the middle of this global pandemic and it is impossible to draw any conclusions with any certainty. However, we can say that it was easier to mobilise and organise a voluntary action response to the pandemic when voluntary action policy and practice was regarded as a central and crucial part of the public response to the pandemic. This proved to be the most effective means of mobilising the huge groundswell of citizen response.

THREE

England

Eddy Hogg, Joanna Stuart, Amy McGarvey and Catherine Goodall

Image 3.1: A Royal Voluntary Service volunteer at a vaccination centre in England

3.1 Introduction

Voluntary action has been a key part of local, regional and national responses to the pandemic in England. From spontaneous highly informal neighbourly help to formal activities coordinated by voluntary and public sector organisations, volunteers have played a vital role during the crisis. The quick, responsive and resilient nature of communities in responding to the pandemic in England has been widely recognised, as too has the role of the voluntary sector in leading the response in many communities (Coutts et al, 2020; McCabe et al, 2020). However, the pandemic has also exposed the legacy of a decade of deprioritisation and disinvestment of the voluntary sector and its infrastructure in England. National government and the sector were on 'shakier ground' at the onset of the pandemic (Dayson and Damm, 2020) and in contrast to the other home nations, voluntary action was not as clearly or distinctly considered within national policy. With this backdrop, our research sought to explore voluntary action responses to the pandemic and understand how policy-making both before and during the pandemic played a role in shaping this response. We ask what the pandemic can teach us about nurturing voluntary action beyond the pandemic and how prepared England is for the future.

The approach we took to develop this understanding was consistent with that taken in the other nations of the UK. First, existing research on voluntary action in England during COVID-19 and over 60 policy documents were identified, collated and reviewed to inform the research. A survey was then developed and shared via a wide range of networks, England-wide, during spring 2021. A total of 127 organisations responded with the majority operating in England, and 17 operating across the UK or internationally. Respondents included:

- local infrastructure organisations such as volunteer centres and Councils for Voluntary Services from every region of England (53 respondents);
- voluntary organisations (47 respondents);
- public sector organisations or bodies, including NHS Trusts (ten respondents);
- volunteering leads in local authorities (eight respondents).

Alongside the survey, we also conducted a series of workshops with stakeholders from infrastructure organisations and volunteer involving organisations to review and provide feedback on the survey findings. A second stage of research was conducted in autumn 2021, engaging with policy-makers to further explore the policy response to the pandemic. This included wider stakeholders, such as volunteer involving organisations, local authorities and infrastructure organisations, to understand the impact of the policy response.

This chapter begins with an analysis of the state of the English voluntary sector, and in particular the infrastructure which supports it, in the period leading up to the onset of the pandemic in March 2020. Next, it looks at the ways in which voluntary organisations and volunteers supported individuals and communities in a diverse range of ways during the pandemic. This section focuses on three key themes: the early stages of the pandemic where much formal voluntary action was paused while informal mutual aid groups developed rapidly; the importance of collaboration and partnership throughout the pandemic; and the focus of English national policy-making on large-scale volunteering schemes. The penultimate section looks forward, asking what we can learn from the response to the COVID-19 pandemic. We conclude by reflecting on how the pandemic has highlighted the strengths of voluntary action and the voluntary sector in England, in particular the importance of collaboration, but also exposed the impact of a decade of limited policy attention and an associated lack of investment.

3.2 The sector in 2020

The past two decades preceding the pandemic saw significant changes in the way in which policy-makers in England approached the voluntary sector and voluntary action. We have seen a shift from the New Labour rhetoric, if not reality, of partnership to the Coalition's more hands-off 'Big Society' approach and more recently to an 'antagonistic collaboration' (Brewis et al, 2021) under the majority Conservative government. Looming large over the latter two periods, since 2010, were substantial funding cuts in the name of 'austerity', which disproportionately impacted local government. In this context, the relationship between the state and voluntary organisations at the national level over the last decade has been described as 'strained', with partnership arrangements between government and voluntary organisations 'scaled back' (Brewis et al, 2021).

Funding from government to the voluntary sector in England reduced significantly over the decade preceding the pandemic. As a proportion of the sector's total income, income from government has fallen continuously since 2008/9 (National Council for Voluntary Organisations, 2021). Significantly for voluntary action in particular, over this period government and other funding for voluntary sector infrastructure was reduced or withdrawn, leading to closures or mergers of organisations and a more fragmented landscape (Macmillan, 2021).

The infrastructure that has survived ten years of austerity varies hugely between different parts of England. This reflects local and regional differences in resourcing of infrastructure for voluntary action, which in many ways mirror other inequalities between areas. Wider research, for example, shows that deprived areas have fewer charities and lower levels of voluntary action (Corry, 2020). The particularly harsh impact of funding cuts on local government – which typically funded local infrastructure organisations – affected the levels of support for infrastructure and the quality of relationships between local government and parts of the voluntary sector (Macmillan, 2021).

At the same time, however, the shift towards public service commissioning led to an increasingly 'complementary relationship' between local government and some local voluntary sector organisations. Many local organisations were already embedded in local government systems and service delivery before COVID-19 hit (Dayson and Damm, 2020). However, the competitive environment commissioning and procurement practices can create has been seen to discourage collaboration and partnership working within the sector (Brewis et al, 2021).

In addition to the uneven patchwork of voluntary sector infrastructure and levels of public and policy engagement with the voluntary sector, responses to previous events and emergencies had prepared some local areas to mobilise voluntary action better than others. In some areas, responding to an emergency like the COVID-19 pandemic was not a first. There are clear and established mechanisms, legislative duties, processes and procedures which govern how local areas should respond to emergencies. This includes the Civil Contingencies Act 2004, the Community Resilience Development Framework and guidance for local authorities in preparing for civil emergencies. Much of this guidance considers the vital role that voluntary action plays in responding to emergencies and sets out how volunteers and voluntary organisations should be engaged. As a result, areas which had experienced recent emergencies, such as localised flooding, often had better integration and more established relationships between Local Emergency Forums or Resilience Partnerships and wider stakeholders.

Where wider voluntary action policy is concerned, recent national policy-making in England has seen voluntary action conceptualised primarily outside of the scope of central government. The government has seen its role as creating the conditions for voluntary action to flourish, albeit with little clarity about what these conditions might be, and at least prior to the pandemic, has not recently taken a directive approach to delivering or supporting voluntary action. This can be observed in the mechanisms for funding and commissioning, which tend to be coordinated through the public, social and private sectors.

The most recent English policy document concerning volunteering is the 2018 Civil Society Strategy. The government's hands-off approach is laid bare, with volunteering positioned within a wider concept of 'civil society' (Bennett et al, 2019). Framing volunteering in this broader and less explicit way differs from the other jurisdictions of the UK considered in this volume, where volunteering is clearly and distinctly considered within national policy, which is then linked to clear action plans. A detailed action plan for the 2018 strategy had not been developed prior to the onset of the pandemic.

In England, at the onset of the pandemic, there was therefore an absence of a cohesive and robust agenda or plan for voluntary action at the national level. Given the levels of disinvestment in local government that occurred alongside this, the local response to the pandemic is remarkable. This response is explored in the next part of this chapter.

3.3 Voluntary action and the sector in the pandemic

Having established the pre-pandemic context for voluntary action in England, we now move on to explore how COVID-19 impacted voluntary action and changed the landscape for volunteers. This section first looks at the initial pandemic response, including the pausing of much existing voluntary action alongside the rapid formation of mutual aid groups in almost every community across England. Next, it explores the ways in which new and existing partnerships and collaborations shaped the voluntary action response. Finally, this section looks at the large-scale, mass volunteering programmes introduced at a national scale by policy-makers in England in response to the pandemic.

3.3.1 Initial changes in voluntary action

The scale and nature of voluntary action has changed significantly and repeatedly over the course of COVID-19. As a result, the pandemic cannot be understood as one homogenous event, but one that changed over time with varying implications for voluntary action.

There were major shifts as individuals, organisations and communities responded to local needs, changing restrictions and evolving personal and organisational circumstances. In particular, the initial lockdown in the early stages of the pandemic was markedly different in character to the long series of easing and tightening of restrictions that followed and continues to the time of writing.

In these early stages, much existing voluntary action was paused. Many volunteers had to step back from their roles, often because of shielding, social distancing requirements or services which had ceased or changed. Wider research reports that in one third of voluntary organisations in England and Wales, the number of volunteers declined between the start of the pandemic and the summer of 2021, while only one in ten reported an increase (Charity Commission, 2021). As a result, the existing formal voluntary sector was working with far less volunteer capacity than usual, at a time when, for many, demand was the highest it has ever been.

However, while much voluntary action through organisations was paused in the early days of the pandemic, huge numbers of people were keen to give their time and talents to support others. The pandemic introduced many new people to voluntary action, with research from Together (2021) finding that around a third of those who volunteered during the first six months of the pandemic were first time volunteers, an estimated 4.6 million people. The furlough scheme in particular was instrumental in enabling many working-age adults to volunteer for the first time.

These new volunteers were involved in a wide range of activities, supporting neighbours, existing voluntary organisations and forming new mutual aid groups, often at extremely local scales and with a neighbourhood or community-level focus. During the first lockdown in March 2020, 4,000 mutual aid groups were registered on the COVID Mutual Aid UK website (Tiratelli and Kaye, 2020). These groups included a huge diversity of activities and approaches, including everything from WhatsApp groups to sophisticated new community organisations. The sizes of these groups varied too, with some having only a handful of members and others having many hundreds (Tiratelli and Kaye, 2020).

Many of the local infrastructure organisations who we surveyed reported this influx of new volunteers during the early stages of the pandemic. Many noted the different profile of volunteers they engaged with during this time, particularly an increase in younger volunteers, including those who were furloughed, who stepped up when older and more vulnerable volunteers had to stand down. Organisations also highlighted that the adoption of more flexible ways of working during COVID-19 has, for some, reduced the bureaucracy of getting involved. However, for some organisations, the pandemic has prompted concerns that it has amplified inequalities in society, in particular for some groups such as disabled volunteers, with organisations unable to support more vulnerable volunteers.

Another aspect of this early stage noted by surveyed respondents was the speed at which individuals and communities stepped up and organised to provide emergency support to members of their community. Organisations shared some of the challenges and tensions this created on the ground. This included an insufficient number of opportunities, due in part to the COVID-19 restrictions, and a lack of capacity to place, manage and support the influx of new volunteers. In some areas, supply of volunteers significantly outstripped demand

and this was cited as a key issue by a number of infrastructure bodies: "We had more than 2,000 people respond to our call for general volunteering support but found the opportunities available were much more limited" (Local infrastructure organisation, East Midlands, survey). Communities and organisations met some of these challenges by creating new roles and opportunities for volunteers. However, this was within the wider context of the considerable challenges being faced by organisations, not least the increase in demand for services and growing financial pressures.

Initially there were some concerns from existing voluntary sector infrastructure organisations that new organisations, such as mutual aid groups, while nobly motivated, were not suitably connected to existing systems and processes, particularly around safeguarding:

> 'Local Mutual Aid set up really fast, iterated really quickly, scaled quickly. It faced challenges from the other agencies, questions about its legitimacy and safety, attempts to marginalise it, but seems to have been very effective in this phase, and we worked to advise and support it, integrate it into the rest of the community response, and connect it with other volunteers in pre-pandemic networks and agencies.' (Local infrastructure organisation, London, survey)

By summer 2020, as restrictions began to ease, many mutual aid groups were increasingly plugged into local voluntary sector networks, while others had faded away: "By [the] end of summer easing levels of activity by mutual aid groups dropped. A couple had disappeared completely. Some were still very active, especially ones that had linked up or even integrated with borough-wide volunteer response" (Local infrastructure organisation, London, survey). As the pandemic moved past these early stages, concerns were raised about the wellbeing of volunteers and burnout (Ellis Paine et al, 2021). The challenges of managing the influx of new volunteers were replaced by other different challenges of sustaining their involvement as furlough came to an end, as well as re-engaging volunteers who had paused their involvement (more on this in section 3.4).

3.3.2 Relationships, collaboration and partnership

Individuals and organisations coming together during COVID-19 has been at the foundation of much of the national and local level response to the pandemic. Collaboration has not, however, been universal and has not been without challenges.

At the national level, Brewis et al (2021, p 153) describe the 'rapidly improvised new relationships' developed early on in the crisis between government and the voluntary sector. Our research showed how new partnerships were formed and voluntary sector organisations shared their knowledge to inform the crisis response at the national level. However, wider research suggests that partnerships faltered as the pandemic progressed and the impact of the pandemic was increasingly being felt by the sector (Macmillan, 2021).

At the local level, research shows how relationships were strengthened and barriers broken down between individuals and organisations during COVID-19, supporting voluntary action and the quick response of communities (McCabe et al, 2020). Multi-agency and cross-organisational working during COVID-19 was a key feature of the response in some areas, representing 'a significant transition away from more traditional silo working towards a place-based response' (Burchell et al, 2020, p 2).

Consistent with these studies, many of the local infrastructure organisations and local authorities who responded to our survey highlighted how they worked collaboratively during the pandemic and the effectiveness of the collective COVID-19 response. This included different types of organisations and agencies working together on the voluntary action response:

'Working at a local level and in partnership across the system has been the key to our success. This needs to be acknowledged nationally – I don't feel it has been.' (Local infrastructure organisation, South West, survey)

'The collaborative, coordinated approach between public and VCS [voluntary and community sector] sectors has to be maintained. The pandemic allowed process, policy and usually stifling "red tape" to be "parked" meaning actions could be taken swiftly and openly between partners to mobilise voluntary support within services and communities. It has to be recognised by central and local government the power and support volunteers and the VCS provided during the pandemic and therefore built upon.' (Local authority, Yorkshire and the Humber, survey)

Other examples in our research included new and strengthened relationships between mutual aid groups – as explored in the previous section – local authorities and local infrastructure. Where it worked well, collaboration led to the effective mobilisation of volunteers and innovative ways of working, with examples of local solutions which will be useful beyond the pandemic.

While some were new, it was – perhaps unsurprisingly – clear that pre-existing relationships, networks and partnerships helped with quick responses to the pandemic. "Two years before COVID[-19] we had already agreed to get involved in the command-and-control structure for an emergency response ... so when we got to COVID[-19] we were very embedded in it all because of those arrangements we had around emergency response" (Local infrastructure organisation, North West, interview). Several other factors were identified as enablers or barriers to collaboration. Having effective lines of communication, mutual understanding and trust in place prior to an emergency situation was seen as key for collaborative working. Technology has also played an important role in keeping volunteers, organisations and agencies connected.

Resources, in particular funding, were also identified as an enabler to collaboration, allowing for innovative collaboration, including between local authorities and the voluntary sector. The VCS Emergencies Partnership was an example of this. This partnership brings together local and national organisations to help deliver a more coordinated response to emergencies and with grant funding from the government the network grew to 30 national organisations and 200 local partners during 2020/1. McMullen and Macmillan (2021, p 13) note how funding through the VCS Emergencies Partnership supported dialogue and collaboration between organisations and 'brought together a diverse range of organisations working in different areas of the country to be able to learn from each other'. Organisations in our study were particularly concerned, however, about a lack of future funding to maintain relationships and the impact this could have.

However, experiences of relationships varied considerably and some organisations reported a lack of joined-up working and missed opportunities in the response, or that the pandemic has brought more competition and less collaboration. Those expressing this felt it to have hampered the voluntary action response to the pandemic. Some experienced disconnection between public agencies responsible for different elements of the pandemic response, poor coordination between local authorities and the voluntary sector in some areas, and less positive relationships between mutual aid groups and local authorities and/or local infrastructure. The impact of this included a slower or more fragmented response and duplication of effort:

'There was a distinct lack of communication between statutory and local organisations leading to (in many cases) duplication. Also, this was mainly a top-down response without considering the grassroots organisations who are in contact with many individuals and groups who were not reached by the other initiatives. Again, a lack of joined up working.' (Local infrastructure organisation, South East, survey)

Many of the examples of disjointed or un-coordinated working that were reported in our research centred on national–local relationships, as many respondents perceived a disconnect between the 'top down' response being driven nationally and what was happening at a local level with the recruitment, mobilisation and management of volunteers. Local infrastructure organisations highlighted that even within a local area, a 'one size fits all' approach was not suitable. National volunteering programmes were cited as examples of this (more on this in section 3.3.3). Some of these issues are likely to be rooted in the disconnection and disenfranchisement that has characterised the relationship between government and the voluntary sector over the last decade.

3.3.3 Mass volunteering programmes

A significant feature of national volunteering policy in England during the pandemic was the focus on large-scale, mass volunteering programmes. The first of these was the NHS Volunteer Responders Programme mentioned previously in this chapter. The programme, a partnership between NHS England and NHS Improvement (NHSE/I), GoodSAM and Royal Voluntary Service (RVS) was originally established to support people who were asked to shield due to underlying health conditions. The programme was designed as an additional service for communities focused on health service activities and was not intended to replace existing local groups or infrastructure (NHS England, 2020a). The programme aimed to match local volunteers with individuals or organisations such as pharmacies through the GoodSAM app. The other large-scale national volunteering scheme focused on the delivery of vaccinations and vaccine boosters, with over 100,000 volunteers recruited to support at vaccine centres (*The Guardian*, 2022), some of whom were matched to roles through the NHS Volunteer Responders Programme.

These programmes were hugely successful in attracting large numbers of willing volunteers. Both too were able to match volunteers with tasks that supported England's response to the pandemic, although with differing levels of success. NHS Volunteer Responders was perceived as effective in our research where the existing local voluntary sector and its infrastructure were less strong. For example, a workshop participant noted that in their local area the programme had been essential, as they had very little local volunteering infrastructure to support the coordination of volunteers at the scale needed during the crisis; a consequence largely of the legacy of regional and local inequality in investment and support for the sector.

The broader impacts of the NHS Volunteer Responders programme are an important part of the picture of how community needs were met during the pandemic. An evaluation of the programme by partner organisation RVS found that the majority of patients supported by the programme felt that their basic needs had been met and it had enabled them to stay at home and stay safe during the early stages of the pandemic (Royal Voluntary Service, 2020).

Not all voluntary sector infrastructure and volunteer involving organisations on the ground shared such positive views. To some, the programme was disruptive of, or distracting from, local arrangements already in place. A number suggested that the programme could have linked better with local arrangements and focused more on the communities with higher levels of demand. The programme and the political rhetoric around it also set high expectations about the numbers of volunteers that could be accommodated by the NHS and reportedly left some volunteers disappointed when they were not matched to tasks or there were delays in being matched: "There was a lot of disruption to local arrangements due to the RVS project, which not only encouraged so many people to volunteer, but set huge expectations of what the NHS could accommodate which could not in any way be fulfilled" (Local infrastructure organisation, London, survey). Despite these challenges, many reflected that the initial outpouring of volunteer support for the Volunteer Responders Programme has helped to raise the profile of voluntary action and the important role of volunteers within communities and among decision makers. Infrastructure organisations similarly reflected on the 'wonderful response' from volunteers to the call for help with the vaccination programme.

The vaccination volunteering scheme was delivered by the NHS in partnership with St John Ambulance, RVS and local infrastructure organisations. This was primarily driven by the health service rather than the government in England and this was seen as a key factor in enabling it to connect and collaborate more effectively with organisations and efforts at the local level compared to other national, more centralised responses. The House of Commons *Lessons Learned* report, for example, points to the openness of the vaccination programme in welcoming volunteer involvement which was seen as starkly different from, for example, the Track and Trace programme (House of Commons Health and Social Care, and Science and Technology Committees, 2021). "In early December we were approached by our clinical commissioning group to recruit non-clinical volunteers to support the surgery vaccination centres – volunteer recruitment was rapid and helped by already having so many links to existing volunteers who had put themselves forward to be COVID-response volunteers" (Local infrastructure organisation, South East, survey).

The outpouring of volunteer support during the pandemic, then, has been facilitated and constrained by a wide range of factors, including English policy approaches to voluntary action and the voluntary sector before and during the pandemic. Consistent with wider research, this has been shaped by the pre-existing environment (Ellis Paine et al, 2021). Where local infrastructure was stronger, it was better able to support newly formed mutual aid organisations, to support an influx of new volunteers and to work in partnership with statutory and voluntary organisations. Where such infrastructure was weaker – either due to cuts over the preceding decade or due to other reasons – there was less support for emergent mutual aid groups, less ability to form and nurture partnerships and more reliance on national volunteer matching schemes.

3.4 Looking forward

In this final section we look to the future, exploring the current and upcoming challenges and opportunities for voluntary action policy and practice. We look at how we might create an environment for voluntary action to thrive beyond the pandemic, and prepare for future challenges.

As we have seen, the pandemic led to fundamental shifts in voluntary action with a significant influx of new and returning volunteers across England as well as the pausing of much existing voluntary action. As restrictions have eased, changed and eased again, volunteer involving organisations have had to carefully consider how to re-engage these existing volunteers in the context of continued uncertainty.

Organisations who participated in our research reported a range of factors they were dealing with, including the wellbeing of volunteers, especially in relation to anxiety about returning to roles; lack of digital skills among volunteers whose roles have shifted online; and the need for existing volunteers to adapt to new ways of working. They noted that some existing but paused volunteers may simply not wish, or not be able, to return.

Organisations have been meeting these challenges with practical measures and a focus on supporting their volunteers. This includes new and refresher training, additional emotional support, peer support through schemes such as volunteer buddies, and the development of micro-volunteering opportunities for people who want to dip their toe back in.

Alongside re-engaging existing volunteers, organisations and communities have also faced challenges with sustaining the involvement of new volunteers. As furlough came to an end and the needs of communities fluctuated, volunteer involving organisations in our research reported losing a number of their new volunteers and many of those active in their communities reportedly stepped back. Sustaining voluntary action has been challenging for organisations and communities, with organisations pointing to a lack of resources and capacity to provide meaningful roles and ongoing support for new volunteers, particularly given the stress that the pandemic has placed on the finances of voluntary organisations. Understanding the different motivations and needs of volunteers during 'crisis' and 'calm' and how best to respond to these to promote a positive volunteering experience needs to be a key part of the approach to sustaining voluntary action. In our research, organisations shared how they are developing new flexible roles, co-developing voluntary activities with volunteers and using technology to engage volunteers.

However, wider research reminds us that sustaining voluntary action may not always be a good thing and we should not 'always assume that more is better' (Ellis Paine et al, 2021). Indeed, our research has shown that during the pandemic, particularly in the early stages, the key issue was less about the 'supply' of volunteers but more about the availability of, and access to, voluntary roles and capacity to support volunteers.

Indeed, the pandemic has brought into sharper focus issues relating to inequalities in access to voluntary action. While the pandemic has broken down some barriers to participation, it has exacerbated others with concerns in our research that some groups will be less likely to return to volunteering including disabled people and those with health conditions. Long before the pandemic, research into voluntary action has consistently highlighted the inequalities in access; those who are more affluent and better educated, for example, are more likely to volunteer, especially where voluntary action takes place in more formal settings (Southby et al, 2019; National Council for Voluntary Organisations, 2021). Events from the past year such as global anti-racism movements and campaigns like #CharitySoWhite in the UK have additionally brought these issues to the fore (Donahue et al, 2020). Looking ahead, organisations saw issues around diversity and inclusion only becoming more important. The need to address digital exclusion was particularly highlighted by organisations in our research, especially given the emergence of more hybrid opportunities. As organisations re-engage existing volunteers and seek to sustain the involvement of newcomers during the pandemic, they must also ensure that they do so in a way which is inclusive and accommodating of the widest possible range of volunteer needs. Organisations in our research gave examples of how they were working towards more inclusive voluntary action, from making onboarding easier to engaging new volunteers through connecting with local groups and communities.

Connecting with others has underpinned much of the voluntary action response to the pandemic and strengthening these connections and relationships will be crucially important for the future of voluntary action. In our research the role of connections between volunteers and organisations and between different organisations/agencies has been particularly highlighted and those involved in our research were taking practical steps to try and sustain collaboration and partnership working to facilitate and support voluntary action to help meet the needs of local communities. This included agencies and organisations working together to create a shared vision for voluntary action, new systems for sharing resources between organisations, including volunteer training, and new ways of working to enable volunteers to move easily between volunteer opportunities and organisations. Collaboration has not however been universal and inequality in access to, and capacity for, collaborative working 'highlights the importance of reaching out beyond existing networks' (McCabe et al, 2021, p 9) as we move beyond the pandemic.

At the national level, there is also a great deal to be learnt from the pandemic with lessons for voluntary action policy-making. During COVID-19 the government in England has been described as acting in isolated ways and an 'absent presence' (Macmillan, 2021), in part a reflection of the absence of a strategic direction or specific agenda for voluntary action pre-COVID-19. Questions about the relationship between the sector, local and national infrastructure, volunteers and the government have been raised in our research, including what role government should, or should not, play in supporting voluntary action: "We've got to be better organised. And, I'll follow whoever is leading … we've got to be organised and we've got to understand who is leading and where does the sector sit in parallel to the state?" (Volunteer involving organisation, national, interview). Recognising this lack of strategic focus and long-term planning for voluntary action in England, a group of voluntary sector organisations are collaborating to develop a ten-year 'Vision for Volunteering'. Driven by a steering group of more than 20 organisations with support from the Department for Digital, Culture, Media and Sport, the work aims to build a clear, ambitious and achievable ten-year plan, with measurable actions.

Indeed, the pandemic has provided a unique opportunity for organisations and communities to think, and perhaps rethink, the voluntary action 'ecosystem' and how it can best thrive. The organisations in our research anticipate challenges ahead. In particular, local authorities, infrastructure and volunteer involving organisations expressed concerns about future funding. Participants emphasised the importance of robust social infrastructure, defined in the wider literature as 'the places and structures and buildings or clubs that enable people to get together, meet, socialise, volunteer and co-operate' (Gregory, 2018, p 11) and the need to invest in this. This is seen as an important part of the government's levelling up agenda and 'how we can collectively strengthen the community and neighbourhood infrastructure needed to build social capital and enable all neighbourhoods to thrive' (Department for Digital, Culture, Media and Sport, 2022). The success of this will be key to creating an empowering and inclusive environment for voluntary action. Achieving this will likely be best done through investment in effective local infrastructure and by understanding what worked before and during the pandemic – relationship building and effective collaboration – rather than through sweeping new initiatives and projects.

3.5 Conclusion

The pandemic has shone a light on the strength of voluntary action and the voluntary sector in England. The impact that volunteers and the sector have had over the course of the COVID-19 pandemic is nothing short of remarkable, particularly given the decade of disinvestment, lack of coordination and absence of strategic direction that preceded it. The community response occurred in spite of, rather than thanks to, the policies around voluntary action that had been pursued in England over the past decade.

Underpinning these responses has been people coming together, connections being made and organisations working collaboratively. The importance of these connections has been a key theme in our research and this chapter. In many places, new partnerships formed and collaboration was facilitated, hastened by urgent need. Yet elsewhere collaboration stalled, hampered by a lack of existing infrastructure. The lack of a pre-existing overarching policy for volunteer involvement – in times of crisis or otherwise – meant that in areas or fields where infrastructure and collaboration was lacking, there was little overall strategy to fall back on. Building, strengthening and sustaining relationships and working collaboratively will be key to creating an environment for voluntary action to flourish beyond the pandemic.

The role of volunteers and the voluntary sector has been widely recognised and celebrated during the pandemic, with the 'significant power of the voluntary sector in supporting people in their local communities' highlighted by the government (Department for Digital, Culture, Media and Sport, 2022). Voluntary action is seen as a key element in the government's levelling up agenda, seen 'as critical to a vibrant and resilient civil society'. If the voluntary sector and volunteers are to play a significant role in national rebuilding – and they surely must – we need far more linked up and long-term thinking. The post-COVID-19 period offers an important opportunity for government and the sector in partnership to develop and deliver a strategic plan for volunteering, setting out the role that the sector, volunteers, government, wider civil society and others can play in creating a vibrant and sustainable environment for voluntary action.

FOUR

Northern Ireland

Denise Hayward, Nick Acheson, Andrew Hanna and Martina McKnight

Image 4.1: Volunteers creating food parcels in Belfast, with Belfast City Council, British Red Cross and SOS Bus

4.1 Introduction

This chapter turns to consider the impact of the COVID-19 pandemic on volunteering in Northern Ireland (NI). The progress of the pandemic and the measures introduced to control and mitigate its effects after March 2020 followed a broadly similar path to the rest of the UK. But the recent history of the jurisdiction and the role of the voluntary sector in that history have been markedly different to the rest of the UK. As the evidence we report will show, the pandemic effect on volunteering has followed a quite familiar pattern, but the capacity and ability of volunteer involving organisations to respond, and the shape and role of third sector infrastructure organisations, have been deeply affected by NI's particular circumstances.

With a population of around two million people, NI's relatively small size, its troubled past and above all its extreme political instability have all had a direct impact on the development of voluntary and community organisations and the voluntary sector more generally (Acheson et al, 2004). The collapse of the NI Executive in February 2022 means that only two administrations since 1965 have served their full term. The emergence of the pandemic as a serious problem in March 2020 occurred only weeks after the government had been restored following a hiatus that had lasted almost three years, during which time there had been policy paralysis and budgetary uncertainty.

At the same time the current landscape of voluntary action in NI has also been deeply shaped by the outsourcing of welfare services to independent providers through competitive tendering, which has led to the disappearance of some long-standing voluntary organisations, the consolidation of others through takeovers and mergers, increased competition for resources, problems of coordination and lack of voice (Hughes, 2019; Hughes and Ketola, 2021). This makes it similar, not only to the rest of the UK (Rees and Mullins, 2016) but also more widely to other countries in Europe (Anheier et al, 2019; Pape et al, 2020).

In this chapter we first explore some of these issues in greater depth and assess the state of voluntary action in NI in 2020 just before the pandemic struck. We then present and discuss our evidence of how the pandemic has impacted on volunteering and the strengths and weaknesses of the response of voluntary organisations in the context of public administration more generally. We then look forward to what this evidence suggests about future directions, before offering some conclusions.

4.2 The sector in 2020

Relative to other UK jurisdictions, NI's voluntary and community organisations are much more closely involved in public administration. At 56 per cent, the percentage of all income from government sources is exactly double the average for the UK where it is 28 per cent (National Council of Voluntary Organisations, 2021; Northern Ireland Council for Voluntary Action, 2021). Both percentages include public service contracts as well as grants. Conversely, the level of support from the general public through donations in NI, at 22 per cent, is less than half that of the UK as a whole where it stands at 48 per cent (National Council of Voluntary Organisations, 2021; Northern Ireland Council for Voluntary Action, 2021).

In the face of political instability, there remains a belief among both civil servants and voluntary sector actors that an important function of civil society in NI is to underpin social stability and support the delivery of effective public administration (Hughes and Ketola, 2021). Every Programme for Government since 1998 has included an endorsement of the importance of voluntary action and a commitment to support it, up to and including the agreement that re-established the institutions of government in January 2020 after a hiatus of almost three years (Hughes and Ketola, 2021).

Generally, this has been interpreted by government as the need to support existing organisations. The documentary evidence suggests there is very little, if any, recognition in policy of a civil society sphere separate from government (Speed, 2021). But through the medium of existing voluntary organisations, it is seen as an important stabiliser, source of social integration and an important means for delivering public policy.

Our evidence on the role of voluntary organisations and the management of the volunteer response to the COVID-19 pandemic as it developed shows how these shared assumptions worked in practice. The view that, fundamentally, government and voluntary action are in the same business, namely the provision of a stable governance regime capable of delivering good social and economic outcomes against a background of deep community divisions and great political instability, was an especially important factor.

The reasons for the high levels of dependence on government and the consequent close relationship with it, arise from a combination of factors including the nature of voluntary action itself in NI as well as a favourable policy environment that dates back to the early 1990s. Then the start of outsourcing health and social care coincided with a change in policy towards community development in the context of the early years of the peace process.

It has long been noted that most voluntary organisations in NI are indigenous to the region (Acheson et al, 2004). Of the 6,122 charities registered with the Charity Commission Northern Ireland (CCNI) in February 2020, only just over were 4 per cent were recorded as also operating in the rest of the UK and 6 per cent in the Republic of Ireland (Northern Ireland Council for Voluntary Action, 2021). The UK figure is certainly an underestimate as thus far the CCNI register does not include charities that are also registered in other jurisdictions. But nevertheless, the numbers of these are likely to be a relatively small proportion of the total. For indigenous charities achieving a level of public support closer to the UK average is simply very difficult. The population is not there to support it. The problem is made more difficult by evidence that despite their charitable aims, most charities in NI remain embedded in one or other of the region's two main communities which most charities tend to reflect and reproduce (Acheson, 2011). In many cases organisations must rely on their 'own' community for support and volunteers.

By the end of 1993, NI had acquired its own strategic policy for engagement with the sector, one that explicitly included community development, establishing a policy unit within government focused on supporting voluntary action, which, with a change in title and departmental home, exists to this day and fulfils largely the same functions (Acheson et al, 2004). The unit continues to fund community development through a scheme administered by the 11 local councils. The era of partnership with government was born and, in an attenuated form, still exists along with many of the assumptions about the value of partnerships for good governance (Hughes and Ketola, 2021). The New Labour era Joint Government Voluntary Sector Forum continues to meet, but above all continuing relatively high levels of government funding of NI-wide infrastructure organisations is evidence of the continuing value placed on voluntary action as a partner of government.

In the New Labour period of direct rule between 2002 and 2007 the balance in government funding shifted decisively towards contracts for outsourced public services. By 2006/7 contracts made up 64 per cent of all income from government, up from 7.7 per cent just five years earlier (Acheson, 2010). Current data on the division between grants and contracts is unavailable, but it is reasonable to assume that the proportion of the latter remains at least as high, if not higher.

This dramatic change in the funding and policy regime produced significant change among larger charities competing for public service contracts. But it is arguable that its reach has been limited. Analysis of income distribution among all NI charities shows this.

Total income for the sector in 2019 was just short of £819 million. But this is not evenly distributed. About 75 per cent of all organisations have incomes of £100,000 a year or less (Northern Ireland Council for Voluntary Action, 2021) and a third of all organisations less than £10,000. All these will either be totally or heavily dependent on volunteers to function. Only 16 per cent of all organisations have incomes over £250,000 a year. So, a minority of organisations scoop up most of that income. In short, most charities are very small and effectively locked out of the funding regime as they lack the resources to engage in competitive tendering and may not wish to; on top of this substrate of voluntarism sits a small minority of professionally staffed charity businesses. Many of these also involve volunteers.

Volunteering thus remains the bedrock of voluntary action in NI. Government policy to recognise volunteering as a social good that should have strategic support dates from 2012. Policy valorisation of volunteering is reflected in continuing support for regional and local volunteering infrastructure organisations. But plans to refresh the policy framework have so far been handicapped by instability in government institutions.

Before the pandemic about 28 per cent of the population volunteered in the previous 12 months; people in paid work volunteered more than those not in paid work and a higher proportion of people volunteered in less deprived neighbourhoods. The three most popular types of organisations for volunteering were church/faith-based organisations and groups (39 per cent), sports organisations (29 per cent) and community and neighbourhood groups (17 per cent) (Volunteer Now, 2021).

4.3 The sector in the pandemic

In this section we summarise our survey and interview data. We also draw on analysis of data gathered from Be Collective, the online volunteer matching platform used in NI (Rutherford and Spath, 2021). The online survey was sent to a sample of 163 organisations in NI identified as having a role in coordinating the response of volunteers to the COVID-19 pandemic. These included all 11 District Councils and the five Health and Social Care Trusts in addition to third sector infrastructure organisations, 60 operating at a local level and 87 across the whole of NI. Unlike the rest of the UK in this study, volunteer involving organisations were not surveyed. Fieldwork took place between 1 April and 1 July 2021 with a response rate of 59 per cent. Those responding to the survey included all 11 District Councils, 6 Health and Social Care Trusts, 36 local organisations and 40 regional organisations. One Trust sent in two responses. Follow-up semi-structured interviews were conducted with five informants in government and third sector roles that were key to the management of the pandemic response. The interviews were carried out between August and September 2021, recorded, transcribed and subject to manual content analysis.

The data are limited both by the survey's focus on the views of infrastructure organisations, and its timing – after the end of the second lockdown and while the mass vaccination programme was still in progress. Although we asked respondents to reflect on three separate time points in the past, their responses are dominated by their thoughts of the period when they completed the questionnaire.

We identified three distinct periods in the pandemic response in NI that we used to measure changes in the pattern of volunteering and the capacity of organisations to manage volunteers as the circumstances changed. These were the first total lockdown March to June 2020, a period of easement of restrictions from July to November 2020 that permitted a greater range of activities and the third period that covered a second lockdown that continued from 26 December 2020 to May 2021. The survey was thus conducted as this second lockdown was ending. In our interviews we asked respondents to reflect on their experience over the same period.

The data reveals the profound impact of the pandemic on the volunteering landscape of NI, illuminating the precarious basis of much voluntary action, and highlights some of the strengths and weaknesses of the relationship between voluntary and community organisations and government agencies. In brief, we found that informal volunteering soared at the start of the pandemic, fell back somewhat as time went on and became better organised as capacity to involve volunteers increased (Rutherford and Spath, 2021). But at the same time activities and services that had depended on long-term volunteer commitment were threatened as people withdrew from volunteering roles; some of these may never recover and there are many voluntary organisations that lack the capacity to adapt to the changing environment.

We look in turn at three areas which are particularly significant. First, the changing nature of the volunteering response to the pandemic as it developed between March 2020 and May 2021; second, the profound disruption caused by the pandemic on volunteer dependent activities and services; and, third, the way the pandemic revealed structural weaknesses in relations between government and voluntary agencies especially in civil contingencies planning, while at the same time demonstrating the importance of existing relationships formed for other purposes. Figure 4.1 summarises respondents' perceptions of how the volunteering response changed through time.

In the initial phase of the pandemic there was an outpouring of offers of help. A majority of respondents reported that informal volunteering and volunteer numbers were higher than pre-pandemic levels. Many offers to volunteer were from people who had never done so in the past. This put severe pressure on the capacity to channel this volunteering effort effectively. Forty per cent of respondents felt that initially they had significantly/rather more volunteers than needed to meet the demand in their areas.

Figure 4.1: Changes in volunteering responses in Northern Ireland

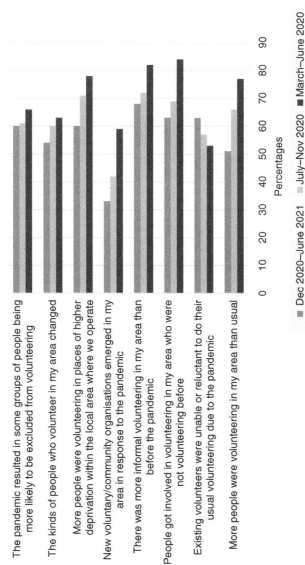

Much of this volunteering was informal. Respondents reported large increases in volunteering at community level without the involvement of formal organisations. Analysis of data from the online volunteer matching platform, Be Collective, shows that as time went on, the numbers of people offering to volunteer fell while at the same time organisations became better at placing those who used the platform to offer their time (Rutherford and Spath, 2021). Although there are no data to measure volunteering response by local area, survey respondents reported that the fall-off in volunteering was uneven. In areas with higher levels of deprivation, it was more difficult to maintain the levels of volunteering. This suggests the influence of factors such as the daily pressures on people who might otherwise volunteer and a lack of organisational capacity locally to support volunteering.

Respondents reported evidence that many people who had been regular volunteers before the pandemic had stopped, either because they were unable to because they were shielding, or because they were unwilling to put themselves at risk of infection in the settings where volunteering typically took place, such as luncheon clubs and charity shops.

While the timing of the survey means that it is difficult to be clear about how long-lasting this effect has continued to be, 94 per cent of respondents expressed a concern about this issue and the next section discusses evidence of its impact. These findings support other research which showed that while overall volunteering had increased during the first year of the pandemic, volunteering with organisations had declined compared to pre-pandemic levels (Volunteer Now, 2021). The trends evident in Figure 4.1 are, arguably, not overly surprising.

The scale of the volunteering response at the outset of the pandemic was quite remarkable, so in most instances, it would have been difficult to increase engagement further. Moreover, sustaining this commitment of time and energy of both individuals and organisations undoubtedly proved challenging given the duration of the pandemic; reinstatement of more normal working patterns, which, for newer, often younger, volunteers, curtailed the time available for volunteering; and the age profile of pre-pandemic volunteers, which, initially, excluded many from volunteering due to shielding, and then, as the pandemic lingered, made them hesitant to return due to ongoing concerns and uncertainty about their safety. The following comments from respondents highlight a number of these factors.

'As an organisation who are volunteer led, a lot of our volunteers are either retired or semi-retired and this put many in the shielding category, so our volunteers went from 68 to about 30 overnight, but our calls for volunteers were answered almost immediately, from male/female, young/old, professional/semi-professional, all walks of life.' (Local infrastructure organisation: respondent 39, survey)

'People on furlough were able to volunteer who couldn't previously because of work commitments. People who usually volunteered, who had health issues, could no longer continue to volunteer as they were shielding.' (Local infrastructure organisation: respondent 61, survey)

'You have to factor in [that] a lot of the normal community and voluntary sector activity was significantly impacted by the pandemic but at the same time the voluntary/community response to assisting vulnerable/isolated people was significant.' (Local Council: respondent 138, survey)

'We found that after the first lockdown many active volunteers during that period were exhausted and glad to step back for a while.' (Local infrastructure organisation: respondent 46, survey)

'Some people were confused about what was and wasn't permissible under the guidance from the Executive so weren't sure if they could or should volunteer. Also, with easement of the lockdown restrictions, people perhaps felt there was less need to be involved in volunteering.' (Local council: respondent 135, survey)

'Some groups availed of funding and developed and delivered community projects to address COVID[-19] issues, but many more groups were unable to deliver projects as their volunteers were shielding. Generally speaking, community groups are managed by older volunteers 50+.' (Local infrastructure organisation: respondent 46, survey)

'A combination of people being worried about the rise in COVID-19 rates and also a sense of there not being the same needs impacted on the volunteering landscape. There was also the sense of things not getting better and the impact of the change in seasons.' (Local council: respondent 135, survey)

As a result of these changes in the pattern of volunteering, our evidence suggests that no form of volunteering escaped being paused at least to some degree and there was no type of volunteering activity respondents judged to be not at risk of ceasing altogether, although there was a spectrum of views as to how likely this would be.

Respondents were most likely to say that all volunteering activities paused, decreased or ceased during the pandemic leading to widespread disruption across all sectors. However, this trend was most noticeable in youth and children's activities outside school (93 per cent), religion (91 per cent) and charity shops (90 per cent), and least evident in politics (69 per cent), health, disability and social welfare (68 per cent) and older people's services (66 per cent).

Respondents were then asked to identify any volunteer programmes/projects that had become inactive in their area during the pandemic and which they felt would restart, and also those programmes/projects that had become inactive which they felt would not recommence and, in the latter instance, why. While a number of respondents indicated in their comments that they were unaware of any specific projects that might not return, others made reference to how their return might be 'cautious' and/or 'gradual' as some groups were "uncertain how to re-establish their operations" or "may struggle to obtain renewed volunteers" as some may have relied on "groups of informal volunteers, people who were on furlough [but had] returned to work and don't have the same time". Other activities mentioned as being at risk included baby clubs, women's clubs, sporting clubs and activities, befriending groups, food banks, shopping assistance, food and medical deliveries and older people's programmes.

Of the paused activities, the least vulnerable to ceasing altogether were activities associated with children's education; the most vulnerable were sports and exercise groups, followed closely by charity shops and youth or children's activities outside school. In the judgement of the respondents, there was not an exact match between the likelihood of pausing and ceasing altogether. The area of volunteering judged most likely to cease altogether were hobby and recreation activities. While somewhat fewer of these had been paused, the evidence suggests that a greater proportion of those that had paused would never restart.

More research is needed to unpack this. We do not know how these impacts vary between richer or poorer, or urban and rural areas for example. Nor do we know very much about the profile of people particularly affected, although the analysis of the Be Collective data suggests disabled volunteers have been slow to return to volunteering (Rutherford and Spath, 2021). It may also be possible that the impact of technology has supported engagement to continue in some areas. In the absence of more fine-grained data, it is difficult to judge what the policy or organisational response should be.

Given the degree of disruption due to the restrictions of the pandemic response and the changing patterns of volunteering, it is remarkable how resilient and adaptable many voluntary organisations have proved to be. Just over three-quarters of respondents said that organisations had changed/refocused the activities they undertake (76 per cent); around two-thirds felt they had provided additional mental health or wellbeing support to volunteers or had moved volunteering activity online (69 per cent and 67 per cent, respectively); while 61 per cent felt that volunteers had been retrained or upskilled to adapt to the changing needs of service users and/or to deliver services differently.

The eruption of spontaneous and informal volunteering as evidenced at the start of the first pandemic lockdown in March 2020 together with the ability of existing organisations and systems to absorb and direct this energy effectively are shaped by policy choices made by governments and existing assumptions about the wider role of volunteering and voluntary organisations in wider processes of public administration. Both what volunteers do and the capacity of voluntary organisations have to be understood in this wider context (Harris, 2020).

The evidence from the interviews suggests that in the initial stages the response to the pandemic in NI was hampered by inadequate emergency response structures that had failed to account for the demands of volunteer mobilisation and the need to manage that successfully in a way that was properly integrated with state bodies.

The interviews drew attention to the poor fit of existing structures managing relations between civil society and government with the demands of managing an emergency response, and second the demands made on these structures by the emergence of mass spontaneous volunteering.

At the start of the pandemic community and voluntary organisations were poorly integrated into existing emergency planning groups set up to deal with civil contingencies. These operated at the level of each of the 11 District Council areas and relations with volunteer mobilising organisations tended to operate at Council level. The extent and effectiveness of these relations varied depending on the Council. Coordinated regionally, these arrangements are overseen by the Executive Office in the NI Government, reporting to the Cabinet Office in London. There is no formal link to other relevant regional government departments, especially the NI Department for Communities which holds the brief for volunteering and community development.

There was widespread recognition that the absence of a formal relationship between these civil continency arrangements with community and voluntary organisations capable of mobilising and managing what was often a very spontaneous volunteer response, was a serious omission. Consequently, as the COVID-19 emergency got underway a structure had to be created using relationships that had been formed for other purposes.

Thus, while the voluntary and community sector had no formalised role in the Civil Contingencies Framework, the Stormont Government department, the Department for Communities, quickly created an 'emergency leadership group' at the start of the first lockdown in March 2020 composed of grassroots and regional third sector leaders as well as key officials from government agencies using existing structures and networks. This group proved very effective in channelling communication between government departments and regional and local voluntary organisations. The value of an effective community and voluntary sector infrastructure with strong pre-existing relations with government was recognised by all the interviewees. "I think having structures. If you didn't have structures, you'd be in real trouble … if you don't have the existing apparatus, you're in a bad spot to begin with" (regional infrastructure organisation, interviews).

4.4 Looking forward

Our evidence has shown the degree of disruption to both patterns of volunteering and the operation of many volunteer-dependent organisations. The experience of the pandemic raised difficult issues around volunteer recruitment and retention, challenging organisations involving volunteers to think creatively about how to fulfil their missions, how they were recruiting volunteers and what they were asking them to do.

The survey data suggest the challenges were putting many organisations under acute pressure and that many of these would require more support to put long-term adaptations in place to address the uncertainties around future patterns of volunteering. Of most concern was the inability or reluctance of former volunteers to return (94 per cent), and the exclusion of particular groups from volunteering (93 per cent); two points that might well be linked. These uncertainties led to high levels of concern over the need to maintain the wellbeing and mental health of volunteers.

Respondents also highlighted a skills gap in organisations' abilities to adapt to what was seen as the inevitable drive to further embed information technology in both service delivery and the management of volunteers. And underpinning this was a strong perception that organisations lacked the resources they needed to manage and support volunteers effectively, either because they were understaffed or lacked the digital expertise to switch to remote working. The evidence suggests that the pandemic experience had served to highlight long-standing problems and accelerate change processes that were already underway.

Respondents commented both on the willingness of people to step up and get involved and on the creativity shown by many community-based organisations. There was ample evidence of the willingness and capacity of local organisations to adapt and deliver what was needed. But in the light of the anxieties expressed about the longer-term impact of the pandemic on patterns of volunteering, new approaches would be needed in the future. One respondent commented:

> 'There remains an untapped willingness among people to help others within their community – an innate human kindness. The volunteering response over the last 12 months suggests that perhaps we need to reframe our "ask" of volunteers in the years ahead; perhaps we have been asking volunteers to focus on things that are important to "government/policy makers" rather than the things that matter within communities – helping those most vulnerable.' (Regional infrastructure organisation, interviews)

To respond, organisations will need training, especially in digital skills and health and safety, improved communication and better coordination especially at local level.

It was also clear that planning will require a much more holistic understanding of volunteering, breaking down traditional ways of thinking about voluntary and community organisations, and formal and informal volunteering, being more aware of the full spectrum of participation people may be able to offer (Williams, 2003, 2011; Woolvin and Harper, 2015; Eden Communities Report, 2021).

In retrospect, the lack of any formal links to local voluntary action in civil contingencies planning at the start of the pandemic seems a gross oversight. This is especially so as the first thing that happened was a spontaneous upswelling of volunteer effort, something that, based on what is already known about disaster planning, could and should have been predicted. Our evidence, although limited, suggests that the performance of NI's 11 District Councils varies a great deal, but they have responsibility for community planning and have access to funds from the regional government to support community development. They also own facilities such as leisure centres and community centres that can be repurposed to support the emergency response.

In the light of the pandemic experience, the problem is now recognised, and steps are being taken to strengthen contingency planning protocols to remedy this. But our evidence also suggests that changing formal structures needs to be accompanied by ensuring local voluntary organisations have the necessary capacity to mobilise and direct volunteers appropriately.

Although often unstated, a strong underlying theme was the availability and appropriateness of funding. Not surprisingly many survey respondents would like to see more of it, but they were also aware that the funds that were available already needed to be streamlined and have a more strategic focus.

Our evidence underlines several key points. First is the fundamental role of volunteering as the bedrock of community responses, but that organisations and the systems in which they operate are not always very good at harnessing it. The pandemic revealed some of the vulnerabilities of volunteering and by extension the organisations that depend upon it. Second, organisations that depend on volunteers need specific kinds of support to recover and adapt. But, third, better policy, structures and planning are needed to deliver this support. Better links to contingency planning and better ways of integrating the specialist knowledge of voluntary organisations, both to bring problems of inequity to the table, and to suggest practical solutions, are needed. It seems especially critical that policy on volunteering and community development is better integrated with the community planning and contingency planning responsibilities of local councils.

4.5 Conclusion

This chapter has reported on evidence of the impact of the COVID-19 pandemic on volunteering and voluntary action in NI. In line with evidence from other parts of the UK, we have illuminated the ways that pandemic-related restrictions had a deep effect on the pattern of volunteering and the activities most dependent on volunteering. It suggests that recovery may be slow and that the capacity of voluntary and community organisations to adapt will require support. Some people who volunteered before the pandemic may never return, and some volunteering opportunities and activities are likely to disappear.

But the chapter also records the truly remarkable spontaneous volunteering response to the onset of the pandemic in 2020. It also records the resilience and adaptability of many organisations, many of which worked in new and unfamiliar ways to respond to the emergency.

A key finding was the lack of fit between policies and administrative arrangements to support volunteering and community development on the one hand and civil contingencies planning on the other. Existing formal partnerships that structure relations between government and voluntary action were out of date and not fit for emergency planning. Political instability has created a lacuna in relevant policy-making. The volunteering strategy for NI has not been refreshed since 2012 and community development has been mired in political arguments about the best ways to address paramilitarism.

However, despite this, the evidence of the speed at which effective structures were created at the start of the pandemic to channel information and marshal resources suggests that continuing government support for voluntary sector infrastructure was vital for this mobilisation of effort. Strong regional organisations with strong relationships with relevant government actors proved crucial. This was replicated at local level in some councils, but the response at that level was uneven and depended on the long-term effectiveness of local community development programmes and the relative openness of councils to dialogue with local community actors.

It is arguable that positive assumptions about the importance of networking and the relevance of fostering good working relations between actors in government and the voluntary sector made up for deficiencies in formal structures. In the absence of appropriate structures, a shared belief in their utility and their value together with continuing government support for a strong regional infrastructure were sufficient to put emergency joint working arrangements in place.

In a UK-wide context, the special circumstances of NI place the relationship between government and voluntary action somewhere between the situation we observe in England on the one hand and Scotland and Wales on the other. Continuing political instability since the 1998 Good Friday Agreement has kept alive the idea of voluntary action as a legitimate source of social stability even if, at the same time, it has left existing volunteering policy out of date and existing structures vitiated. The experience of the pandemic shows the urgent need to address this. First, to ensure that all those organisations most at risk from the disruption it caused to volunteering have the support they need; and, second, that the role of volunteering is recognised in emergency planning and structures put in place to give that effect.

FIVE

Scotland

Matthew Linning and Debbie Maltman

Image 5.1: Volunteer Edinburgh's Community Taskforce volunteers

Note: Volunteers supported people impacted by COVID-19 with practical tasks such as shopping delivery and dog walking

5.1 Introduction

Volunteering in Scotland, as in all nations of the UK, has been significantly impacted by COVID-19. As restrictions and subsequent lockdowns were implemented (see Image 5.1), organisations and individuals came together at pace to develop solutions and support those most in need. A new 'can do' attitude brushed aside a lot of the bureaucratic and other barriers to 'make change happen'.

A distinctive characteristic of the Scottish volunteering landscape which helped to facilitate this nationwide response was the embedded commitment to volunteering from key organisations at both national and local levels. Long before the outbreak of COVID-19 the Scottish Government has provided policy and funding support for volunteering channelled through its Third Sector Unit. This annual funding supports the work of Volunteer Scotland, the Scottish Council for Voluntary Organisations (SCVO) and a network of 32 Third Sector Interfaces (TSIs), one for each of Scotland's local authority areas. This infrastructure and the underpinning relationships were critical in supporting Scotland's response to the volunteering challenges of COVID-19.

However, as in the rest of the UK, it was the volunteer involving organisations (VIOs) and volunteers themselves which delivered the vital support 'on the ground'. People came forward to help out who had not previously volunteered, and hundreds of new mutual aid groups were formed at short notice. The impact of COVID-19 was seismic in terms of its once-in-a-lifetime impact on volunteering engagement.

To help understand these impacts Volunteer Scotland joined a collaborative research study entitled 'Mobilising Voluntary Action Across the UK'. The Scottish report entitled 'The Road to Recovery: Lessons Learned from Scotland's Volunteering Response to COVID-19' was one of four national reports delivered as part of this study funded by the Economic and Social Research Council (Volunteer Scotland, 2022). Drawing upon a rich evidence base the findings demonstrate the remarkable community and volunteering contribution, which has been an integral element of society's multilayered response to the COVID-19 crisis. Although inevitably some mistakes were made along the way, the far greater impact was the introduction of new structures, new models of working, new and stronger relationships, new ways of supporting volunteering, and new volunteer roles.

This chapter explores the actual and projected impact of COVID-19 on volunteering in Scotland during the pandemic and over the longer term. A particular focus is on the identification of lessons learned: not just the challenges that need to be addressed as part of Scotland's recovery and preparedness for future crises, but also the important opportunities that can be capitalised upon to enhance the contribution of volunteering in 'steady state'. This learning represents a golden opportunity to secure a lasting volunteering legacy from COVID-19.

This chapter is structured into four sections: the Scottish context pre-pandemic; the impact of COVID-19 on the third sector and volunteering; the lessons learned to help inform the future of volunteering in Scotland; and the conclusions to help support 'evidence into action'. Figure 5.1 gives the COVID-19 timeline in Scotland.

The following terms need to be explained, especially for non-Scottish readers:

• TSIs provide a single point of access for support and advice for the third sector within each of Scotland's 32 local authority areas.
• Infrastructure organisations support and/or coordinate volunteering across an area or sector and include local organisations such as TSIs and local authorities; and national organisations such as Volunteer Scotland and SCVO, and sectoral umbrella bodies.

Figure 5.1: Scottish COVID-19 timeline

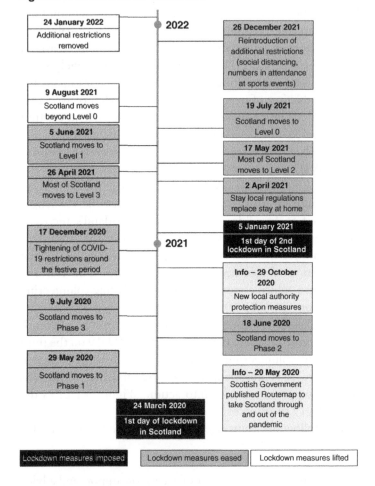

5.2 The Scottish context before COVID-19

The objectives of this section are twofold: to present a volunteering baseline against which to measure the impact of COVID-19; and to review the volunteering and resilience policy context relevant to Scotland's third sector and volunteering response.

5.2.1 Scottish volunteering context

Based on the Scottish Household Survey (SHS) data in 2018, 48 per cent of adults in Scotland volunteered either formally or informally, equivalent to 2.2 million volunteers and 361 million hours of help. The value to the Scottish economy was £5.5 billion. Of this total volunteering contribution, the formal volunteering participation rate was 26 per cent, valued at £2.3 billion; and the informal volunteering participation rate was 36 per cent, valued at £3.2 billion (Volunteer Scotland, 2019).

To help understand the impact of COVID-19 on volunteering in Scotland, Volunteer Scotland commissioned Ipsos MORI to undertake a survey of adult volunteering participation before and during the pandemic. For the 12 months prior to the outbreak of COVID-19, April 2019 to March 2020, the total adult volunteering participation rate was 45 per cent, which was a similar figure to the SHS 2018 data (Volunteer Scotland, 2020a).

5.2.2 Scottish volunteering policy

Reflecting Scotland's National Performance Framework policy priorities (Scottish Government, 2022a), the Scottish Government has published two strategic guidance documents that are relevant to the third sector's response to COVID-19 in Scotland: the first focuses on volunteering and the second on resilience (see section 5.2.3).

'Volunteering for all: Our national framework' was published by the Scottish Government in April 2019, providing new guidance on Scotland's volunteering policy priorities. The development of the 'Outcomes Framework' was led by the Scottish Government but was co-produced with a wide-ranging stakeholder group with expertise and a vested interest in volunteering (Scottish Government, 2019b). The document reflects the strong commitment to collaborative working between the Scottish Government and key partners on issues relating to volunteering.

Volunteering can be interpreted as supporting all 11 National Performance Framework Outcomes (Scottish Government, 2022a), either directly or indirectly, but four have been prioritised in the 'Outcomes Framework' because of the perceived strength of the contribution from volunteering: 'we live in communities that are inclusive, empowered, resilient and safe; we are well educated, skilled and able to contribute to society; we tackle poverty by sharing opportunities, wealth and power more equally; and we are healthy and active' (Scottish Government, 2019b, p 30).

To assist in the roll-out and practical application of the Framework, the Scottish Government, in partnership with Volunteer Scotland and a wide range of partners, co-produced 'Scotland's Volunteering Action Plan', published in June 2022 (Scottish Government, 2022d). This work was guided by five volunteering outcomes: volunteering and participation is valued, supported and enabled from the earliest possible age and throughout life; volunteering in all its forms is integrated and recognised in our lives through local and national policy; there is an environment and culture which celebrates volunteers and volunteering and all of its benefits; the 'places and spaces' where we volunteer are developed, supported and sustained; and there are diverse, quality and inclusive opportunities for everyone to get involved and stay involved.

Although there is a strong policy direction in Scotland related to volunteering, with a particular focus on its contribution towards the Scottish Government's National Performance Framework and specific National Outcomes (Scottish Government, 2022a), there are no overt resilience or 'emergency-type' volunteering policy priorities. However, the volunteering outcomes are supportive in broad terms of a resilience response.

5.2.3 Scottish resilience policy and structure

A key driver of resilience planning in Scotland is the National Performance Framework Communities' Outcome, 'We live in communities that are inclusive, empowered, resilient and safe' (Scottish Government, 2019b, p 30). Community resilience is defined by the Scottish Government as: 'Communities and individuals harnessing resources and expertise to help themselves prepare for, respond to and recover from emergencies, in a way that complements the work of the emergency responders' (Scottish Government, 2019a, p 2). It is based on a culture of preparedness, in which individuals, communities and organisations take responsibility to prepare for, respond to and recover from emergencies. The approach recognises the diversity of individuals in a community and that this diversity affects the way emergencies impact at community, individual and household levels. Hence, different emergencies have the potential to make different people vulnerable in different ways. The importance of understanding this diversity and recognising that vulnerability is dependent on context is discussed in 'Preparing Scotland: Care for people affected by emergencies' (Scottish Government, 2020d).

The Civil Contingencies Act 2004 (Contingency Planning) (Scotland) Regulations 2005 provides the foundation for resilience planning in Scotland, including the legal obligations of statutory responders and community risk registers (Scottish Government, 2004). The formal resilience structure includes the Voluntary Sector Resilience Partnership which has been in existence for over ten years (Volunteer Scotland, 2022, p 56).

The practical application of the 2004 Act relating to the Voluntary and Community Sector (VCS) is articulated in the Scottish Government's publication 'Building resilient communities' (Scottish Government, 2019a). This provides good practice guidance for responders to maximise the effectiveness of their work with individuals, community groups, private sector businesses and third sector organisations (TSOs), to help make themselves more resilient.

However, pre-COVID-19 infrastructure organisations' awareness of, and involvement in, resilience planning varied significantly: 37 per cent rated their level of awareness of resilience planning as 'limited' or 'none' and 42 per cent rated their level of involvement as 'limited' or 'none' (Scottish Government, 2022b). Perhaps unsurprisingly, the awareness and involvement of local authorities in resilience planning was much higher than TSIs.

Based on feedback from the Scottish Government and the SCVO this variation in the involvement in resilience planning was recognised as an issue, and was being actively addressed pre-pandemic (Volunteer Scotland, 2022).

5.3 The Scottish third sector in the pandemic

In considering the impact of, and response to, COVID-19 on the third sector in Scotland three distinct groups are considered separately: volunteers, VIOs and infrastructure organisations, including Scottish Government.

5.3.1 The volunteer response

Volunteer participation

There are two complementary surveys which highlight marked changes in volunteering participation during COVID-19: Ipsos MORI and the SHS 2020. The Ipsos MORI survey is specific to the first lockdown and asked a representative sample of 1,014 Scottish adults whether they had given any unpaid help between March and June 2020 (Volunteer Scotland, 2020a). Total volunteering participation increased from an annual rate of 45 per cent of adults in Scotland pre-pandemic to 74 per cent during March–June 2020. Volunteers were mainly keeping in touch with people who were isolated and lonely, and undertaking tasks in response to the immediate crisis. There was also an increase in volunteer engagement by younger adults and new or lapsed volunteers during this period (Volunteer Scotland, 2020a).

The majority of the SHS 2020 interviews were conducted between January and March 2021 and, given its focus is on volunteering participation over the previous 12 months, it provides a good insight into adult volunteering participation during the first year of COVID-19 (Scottish Government, 2022c). Like the Ipsos MORI data, total volunteering participation increased significantly from 48 per cent in 2018 to 64 per cent in 2020. However, this aggregate increase masks significant differences between formal and informal volunteering participation. The former has remained static at 26 per cent for the last three years, 2018–20, with the decline in more traditional formal volunteering during COVID-19 being compensated by an increase in mutual aid volunteering. In contrast, informal volunteering participation increased from 36 per cent in 2018 to 56 per cent in 2020. This major increase in informal volunteering reflects how people came together to help each other in their immediate neighbourhoods, which is reflected in the types of volunteering support provided, especially during lockdowns:

- Keeping in touch with someone who is at risk of being lonely: adult volunteering participation up from 18 per cent in 2018 to 69 per cent in 2020.
- Doing shopping, collecting pension, benefits or paying bills: up from 12 per cent to 51 per cent.
- Providing transport or accompanying someone away from home: up from 9 per cent to 20 per cent.
- Routine household chores: up from 11 per cent to 19 per cent.
- Providing advice or support with letters or forms or speaking with others on someone else's behalf: up from 6 per cent to 16 per cent.

To help interpret this survey data and to understand the 'volunteer voice' this section includes indirect evidence on volunteering from surveys and other evidence sources, which reflect the views of VIOs and infrastructure organisations rather than the volunteers themselves. Mutual aid and informal volunteering are discussed in this section; formal volunteering is discussed in section 3.2.

Mutual aid

Mutual aid provided an important contribution during COVID-19 in Scotland, especially in supporting the crisis response during lockdowns. The evidence indicates that mutual aid decreased between lockdowns – July to November 2020 – before increasing during the second lockdown, but not to the same level as the first lockdown. Key attributes included speed of response for the crisis needs of food, transport, shopping and shelter; community connectivity, accessibility and local knowledge; ability to support both those shielding, and those vulnerable but not shielding; reaching those in need in areas of deprivation; and large group membership providing ready access to volunteers (Curtin et al, 2021; Scottish Government, 2022b).

However, infrastructure organisations identified two main areas of concern. First, that many mutual aid groups did not have adequate safeguarding or confidentiality measures to ensure protection for people receiving support (60 per cent agreed/strongly agreed); and second, that mutual aid groups were not always able to provide volunteers with adequate training, guidance and support for their role (56 per cent agreed/strongly agreed) (Scottish Government, 2022b).

Informal volunteering

Qualitative evidence reinforces the findings from the SHS 2020 quantitative data on the importance of the informal volunteering contribution (Scottish Government, 2022b). Informal volunteers were primarily involved in keeping in touch with neighbours who were at risk of being lonely and helping to meet the immediate support needs of those in their local area. The Scottish Government survey rated the contribution of informal volunteers highly: 90 per cent of infrastructure organisations agreed that informal volunteers had an important role in combatting social isolation in their local area during COVID-19; 87 per cent agreed that neighbours helping each other through informal volunteering was an essential complement to formal volunteering; and 85 per cent agreed that informal volunteering had strengthened community spirit and identity (Scottish Government, 2022b).

5.3.2 The volunteer involving organisations' response

VIOs were impacted in a multitude of ways during COVID-19. The imposition of the first lockdown on 24 March 2020 resulted in a stay-at-home order, face-to-face services stopping, the furloughing of staff, shielding of vulnerable groups and charity retail operations being paused, all of which severely impacted VIOs' business operations.

The Office of the Scottish Charity Regulator's surveys in May and November 2020 provide hard-hitting evidence on how Scotland's charities were impacted (Volunteer Scotland, 2021). In the first lockdown over three-quarters of charities had to postpone or cancel planned work, with over a third having to suspend their operations altogether. This evidence is corroborated by the TSI Scotland Network survey which showed that 30 per cent of TSOs had stopped 'meaningful delivery' by June 2020 (Volunteer Scotland, 2020b).

Furthermore, although there was a measurable improvement in business operations between May and November 2020, a very significant proportion of charities were still being adversely affected, despite the fact that restrictions on daily life were much reduced and government emergency funding was starting to come onstream (Volunteer Scotland, 2021).

Directly linked to the impact of COVID-19 on VIOs' business operations is the impact on their finances. Just over a half of charities lost income from fundraising in the first lockdown; with this position deteriorating between May and November 2020, from 51 per cent of charities adversely affected to 56 per cent. There were also adverse financial impacts from lost trading, other income sources and short-term risks to charity reserves. Furthermore, these impacts were not considered short term (Volunteer Scotland, 2021).

These business impacts, combined with COVID-19 restrictions such as social distancing and shielding, resulted in a major contraction in the number of formal volunteers during the first lockdown and, to a lesser extent, the second lockdown. Over the period March 2020 to May 2021, 58 per cent of VIOs reported a decrease in their number of volunteers, 27 per cent an increase, and 15 per cent reported no change. VIOs also identified a series of problems in the involvement of volunteers, these challenges being rated as either a 'major challenge' or 'some challenge': volunteers' lack of digital skills (58 per cent of VIOs); the challenge of making volunteering inclusive (46 per cent of VIOs); volunteers' fatigue/burnout and other wellbeing issues (47 per cent of VIOs); reduction in volunteers due to home schooling/caring responsibilities (47 per cent of VIOs); and a lack of staff support and equipment (44 per cent of VIOs) (Scottish Government, 2022b).

In addition to curtailing volunteer services and making them COVID-safe, the most significant change was the adaptation of volunteer services and, specifically, the use of phone/digital platforms, with 56 per cent of VIOs moving some or all of their activities online. However, the switch to digital was no universal panacea due to the lack of volunteers' digital skills; the exclusion of beneficiary groups such as older adults, disabled people and those excluded due to the cost or lack of equipment; and the fact that many services are not suited to online delivery. Face-to-face engagement is critical for so many services. VIOs also provided training support to existing volunteers to help them adapt to the new or evolved service delivery models (43 per cent of VIOs); provided remote training and onboarding support for new volunteers (37 per cent of VIOs); and provided additional mental health and wellbeing support for their volunteers (42 per cent of VIOs) (Scottish Government, 2022b).

During the first lockdown the biggest immediate societal concerns identified by TSOs were mental health (86 per cent of TSOs) and loneliness (83 per cent of TSOs). COVID-19 has exacerbated these challenges, which were already major issues pre-pandemic. The second main category of societal needs identified by TSOs related to financial hardship, unemployment and poverty. These adverse impacts have put additional pressures on the third sector to not only support existing beneficiaries with their pre-pandemic needs, but also in supporting the additional needs of existing and new beneficiaries caused by COVID-19 (Volunteer Scotland, 2020b).

All of these impacts affected VIOs' ability to meet the needs of beneficiaries and service users throughout the pandemic. By May 2021 62 per cent of VIOs were able to meet 'all' or 'most' requests for support; a further 23 per cent of VIOs were able to meet some requests for support, but significant needs were not being met; while 9 per cent of VIOs were being faced with requests for support which were much higher than their response capacity, and many requests were not being met (Scottish Government, 2022b).

5.3.3 Scottish Government and infrastructure organisations' response

This subsection focuses on three aspects: the resilience response during COVID-19; the role and coordination of infrastructure organisations; and Scottish Government-led support through Scotland Cares and funding provision.

The resilience response

During COVID-19 the voluntary sector's involvement in Scottish resilience planning and operational support was enhanced through the following measures: an expansion in the membership of the Voluntary Sector Resilience Partnership; setting up of the VCS Advisory Group; and Foundation Scotland launching the 'Response, Recovery and Resilience Fund' in partnership with the National Emergencies Trust (Volunteer Scotland, 2022).

During the pandemic the effectiveness of the resilience response was rated highly by 64 per cent of infrastructure organisations, which was due to good communication, coordination of partners, effective partnership working and shared learning (Scottish Government, 2022b). Suggested enhancements include more effective engagement of the third sector, especially TSIs; an increased focus on the community response and addressing longer-term societal challenges; and recognising and supporting the mutual aid response (Volunteer Scotland, 2022).

Role and coordination of infrastructure organisations

Support provided by infrastructure organisations during COVID-19 included the registration of volunteer sign-ups; the matching of volunteers to opportunities; provision of guidance and information; funding assistance and advice; and setting up new services, programmes or groups. They also provided support outside formal volunteering with 88 per cent of infrastructure organisations supporting mutual aid groups and 69 per cent supporting informal volunteering, which represents a major change in focus compared to pre-COVID-19, where formal volunteering was the sole priority (Scottish Government, 2022b).

Local coordination of the volunteering response between key partners was rated highly, with 75 per cent of infrastructure organisations assessing the coordination between TSIs and local authorities as either 'excellent' or 'good'. The equivalent figure for coordination with other partners locally was 79 per cent. However, 44 per cent of respondents stated that there has been 'limited' or 'no' coordination between their organisation and national partners (Scottish Government, 2022b). Going forward, it will be important to build on the positive examples of coordination and collaboration triggered by COVID-19, embedding these new relationships across all local authority areas.

Scottish Government-led support through Scotland Cares and funding provision

On 31 March 2020 the Scottish Government launched its Scotland Cares campaign which invited people to register their interest to volunteer via the Ready Scotland website. The objective was to provide one place for potential volunteers to go, to sign up and to be redirected to local organisations so that if and when they were needed that need could be expressed and met locally. People could sign up via Volunteer Scotland or British Red Cross links and these sign-ups were matched with local needs in a range of organisational settings. The campaign was paused on 1 May 2020 because the supply of volunteers outstripped demand. Total volunteer sign-ups were over 60,000, comprising 35,262 sign-ups to Volunteer Scotland to support charities and community groups and 25,172 sign-ups to the British Red Cross to support public services. Since that date there has been no requirement to restart the campaign given the sufficient supply of volunteers locally (Scottish Government, 2022b).

There were consistent views on the positive aspects of Scotland Cares from infrastructure organisations, the Scottish Government and SCVO. This included the 60,000 sign-ups which demonstrated the desire from the people of Scotland to help out by volunteering; the increased volunteering profile which the campaign generated through mainstream media, which would be difficult to replicate under normal non-crisis conditions; and the campaign's role in harnessing and coordinating the community response (Volunteer Scotland, 2022).

Notwithstanding these positive impacts there were three key linked problems. First, the demand–supply imbalance due to the relatively small number of immediately available formal volunteering opportunities during the first lockdown compared to the large number of sign-ups, which meant that most applicants did not get the chance to volunteer. Second, the heavy workload involved in the administration of the Scotland Cares sign-up and registration process; and lastly, the 'window of interest' from volunteer sign-ups was limited, especially after the first lockdown when people came off furlough and started to return to work (Volunteer Scotland, 2022).

Funding support for the third sector was a critical component of the Scottish Government's response to COVID-19, which included circa £100 million to support the third sector, overseen by the Third Sector Unit of Scottish Government and administered by key funding partners. Not only did this funding help to sustain and support service delivery of TSOs, but it also helped to support the key role of volunteers. Positive aspects of the funding support provided include effective collaboration by funding partners, the early provision of funding, real-time learning, flexibility and risk taking, and centralised funding information. More time for planning was the area that infrastructure organisations highlighted as an area for improvement (Volunteer Scotland, 2022).

5.4 Looking forward

Important lessons have been learned from the impact of COVID-19 on the third sector in Scotland. The challenges faced by infrastructure organisations, VIOs, volunteers and beneficiaries have acted as a catalyst for positive change. To help ensure that the new ways of working are recognised, supported and developed – not just for the ongoing COVID-19 response, but to foster and support volunteering post-pandemic, Volunteer Scotland has developed a 'Routemap to Improvement' – see Figure 5.2 (Volunteer Scotland, 2022).

Figure 5.2: Routemap to Improvement: A Learning Journey

A. Policy and Planning	'The foundations'
• Voluntary and Community Sector Resilience	• Volunteering for All Outcomes Framework
(National direction and local implementation)	

Implications →

B. Leadership	'The catalyst for change'
National Level ↔ Local Level ↔ Community Level	

Implications →

C. Expected responses	'What happens in a crisis'
• Funding £s • Partnership & collaboration • Information, guidance & training	• Addressing societal needs • Campaigns (Scotland Cares) • Informal volunteering – individuals' responses

Implications →

D. Unexpected responses	'The unplanned'
• Digital uptake • Mutual aid response • Community engagement	• Recognition & celebration • Challenges to inclusive volunteering • 'Just do it'

Implications →

E. Formal volunteering priorities & needs	VIOs and volunteers 'The agents of change'
VIO priorities • Addressing societal challenges • Embedding digital models • Volunteer recruitment • Volunteer management • Volunteers' health & wellbeing • Youth volunteering	**Support needs** • Infrastructure orgs' support • Funding provision • Training support • Partnership working • Recognition & celebration • Inclusive volunteering

Implications →

Learning (vertical, left axis)

F. Informing Scotland's Volunteering Action Plan (vertical, right)

The 'Routemap' also identifies how we can improve through learning from our mistakes which will help us to maximise the contribution of volunteering to society. The danger is that if we don't act now a lot of this good practice and lessons learned may be lost as we revert to the old 'business as usual' model.

There are five overarching elements underpinning Scotland's response to COVID-19 which we need to learn from: policy and planning, leadership, the expected and unexpected responses, and formal volunteering priorities and needs.

5.4.1 Policy and planning

'Scotland's Volunteering Action Plan' will assist in addressing the requirement for more detailed volunteering priorities for Scotland relevant to the recovery from COVID-19, addressing future crises and volunteering in the longer term (Scottish Government, 2022d).

There is also a strong platform to build on the positive progress in resilience planning and operation during COVID-19. This includes a continuation of the integration of the voluntary and community sector alongside statutory responders such as local authorities, power companies, NHS and emergency responders; embedding the voluntary and community sector more effectively and consistently in Local Resilience Partnerships and Groups – particularly the TSIs; and reviewing the need for resilience planning as an integral element of Scottish Government's funding agreements with TSIs.

5.4.2 Leadership

There is an opportunity for Scottish Government and national partners to review how to further improve national level leadership of volunteering in Scotland, including roles and responsibilities during a crisis.

At the local level TSIs' leadership role for volunteering is now much more widely recognised by local authorities and this needs to be embedded across all areas. Also, TSIs and local partners have the opportunity to review their experience from the pandemic in facilitating community-led action, to identify and share good practice.

5.4.3 Expected responses

'Expected responses' are defined as the main categories of response that one can depend on during a major crisis: funding, information, guidance, working together, addressing major needs, and so on. These all came to the fore during COVID-19 and if there was another crisis tomorrow, we would have confidence that similar categories of response would occur. However, a series of suggestions to enhance performance were identified.

Funding – there is an opportunity to bring together a representative group of funders to discuss how to improve the awareness and understanding of volunteering by funders, the resources required to support volunteers and volunteering, and the protocols for the allocation and distribution of funding. Consideration also needs to be given to the funding needs of infrastructure organisations, reflecting the increased recognition of the vital role they have played during the pandemic.

Partnership and collaboration – suggestions include strengthening specific local authority areas where progress during COVID-19 has been weaker; building on the positive collaboration between TSIs and local authorities in areas such as Community Planning Partnerships; consolidating the improved functioning of TSI Scotland Network; and enhancing communication between national and local partners relevant to the third sector.

Information and guidance – Scotland's information and guidance response could be improved both nationally and locally through the provision of clearer guidelines on the involvement of volunteers throughout all phases of a crisis; ensuring that the new-found recognition of informal volunteering in a crisis is retained and that appropriate support is provided; and through more effective information and data sharing between partner organisations at all levels.

Training provision – VIOs identified specific areas of support for their provision of training, including funding support to help them cover costs in areas such as online/remote volunteering; the creation of new online training products for VIOs; and training provision which is complementary to the standards of 'Investing in Volunteers' and 'Volunteer Friendly'.

Addressing societal needs – COVID-19 has demonstrated how important formal volunteering is in helping to address society's more complex long-term challenges such as mental health, loneliness and poverty, and this contribution should be recognised and supported. Assisting VIOs to deliver inclusive volunteering outcomes will also help address these societal needs.

Scotland Cares – the following factors should be reviewed by the Scottish Government and key partners to inform future initiatives: the involvement of organisations with specialist knowledge on volunteering including Volunteer Scotland, the TSI Scotland Network and the Scottish Volunteering Forum; the efficacy of an appraisal process to inform the development of volunteer engagement campaigns; how the effective partnership working associated with Scotland Cares could be capitalised on for future campaigns, events and relationships more generally; how best to manage volunteers' expectations when there are significant variables in campaigns of this nature; and the importance of acknowledging the contribution of volunteers who are not part of a campaign.

Informal volunteering – 'acknowledging and supporting informal volunteering' was the third most frequently cited priority by infrastructure organisations to support Scotland's recovery from COVID-19. Notwithstanding the difficulty in supporting individuals rather than organisations, there are implications from COVID-19 which need to be considered: the recognition of the role and contribution of informal volunteering by infrastructure organisations; the scope to support informal volunteers during a crisis; and the opportunity to stimulate informal volunteering through enhanced community engagement.

5.4.4 Unexpected responses

'Unexpected responses' are defined as the responses to COVID-19 that people did not see coming and could not realistically have been predicted in advance. They have introduced innovative ways of collaborating, working together and delivering services with the potential for long-term legacy impacts. However, some unexpected responses have also presented challenges which need to be addressed.

Digital uptake – the uptake of digital technology and its application in innovative ways through video platforms such as Zoom and Teams, to social media platforms and the 'good old phone' have been transformational in the support of volunteers and the delivery of their services. However, support is required to help embed digital good practice, while mitigating its limitations.

Mutual aid groups – they formed at pace and are ideally suited to supporting a crisis resilience response. However, for many groups their longer-term role in 'steady state' is more uncertain. Already there is evidence of many groups moving to community support pages on Facebook, becoming dormant or ceasing to operate altogether. However, this should not be viewed as a negative. Their very strength is their ability to come together and to act quickly in response to crises.

Community engagement – society's response to COVID-19 demonstrated the positive community level impacts with people looking out for each other, and people developing new connections and better relationships. The mutual aid and informal volunteering response was critical in achieving this strengthened community spirit and identity. Capitalising on these COVID-19 impacts, infrastructure organisations are keen to build stronger and more resilient communities.

Recognition and celebration – there is an opportunity to build on the increased profile of volunteering and the recognition of its importance to society. This is not just about further increasing the recognition and celebration of volunteers by VIOs, but also 'influencing the influencers' such as the Scottish Government, national, regional and local organisations.

Inclusive volunteering – infrastructure organisations identified a range of support measures to tackle volunteering barriers exacerbated by COVID-19 including the re-establishment of volunteering programmes for people with higher support needs; working with minority communities; making volunteering opportunities more welcoming and inclusive; and infrastructure organisations and community groups delivering a more joined-up approach to support and develop inclusive volunteering.

'Just do it' – so much has been achieved so quickly compared to what typically happens in 'steady state'. This begs the question as to why the attributes of the 'just do it' attitude cannot be retained beyond COVID-19 as a key lasting legacy. There is an opportunity to embed the attributes of this can-do business philosophy and combat the pressures for a return to the old 'business as usual' model.

5.4.5 Formal volunteering priorities and support needs

In the Scottish Government survey VIOs identified specific volunteering priorities such as addressing societal challenges; capturing the best of what digital has conferred and mitigating its limitations; volunteer recruitment to re-engage former volunteers and attract new volunteers; volunteer management; volunteers' health and wellbeing; and youth volunteering (Scottish Government, 2022b).

To help them deliver these priorities, VIOs need support from the Scottish Government, national bodies, TSIs and local partners in the following areas: funding support, especially for volunteer management and coordination roles; improved collaboration and joint working between infrastructure organisations, nationally and locally; increased recognition of the contribution of volunteering by the Scottish Government and partners; and support in helping to tackle the barriers to more inclusive volunteering outcomes (Scottish Government, 2022b; Volunteer Scotland, 2022).

5.5 Conclusion

The evidence presented in this chapter demonstrates the strength of Scotland's third sector and volunteering response to COVID-19. Individual volunteers stepped forward, with almost three-quarters (74 per cent) of Scottish adults volunteering during the first lockdown (Volunteer Scotland, 2020a). Informal volunteering increased and played a critical role in supporting those at risk of social isolation, hundreds of mutual aid groups formed at pace to support local communities, while at the same time formal volunteering discovered new ways to deliver volunteering support in the face of major challenges.

VIOs were adversely impacted by stay-at-home orders, face-to-face services stopping, the furloughing of staff, shielding of vulnerable groups and charity retail operations being paused, all of which severely impacted on VIOs' business operations. Despite these challenges VIOs adapted during COVID-19 to ensure that their beneficiaries and service users were supported, for example through the application of digital technology.

Similarly, infrastructure organisations and the Scottish Government adapted the ways in which they worked to support the sector. For example, infrastructure organisations helped support mutual aid groups and provided guidance for informal volunteers in addition to their support for VIOs and formal volunteering. The Scottish Government made changes to resilience structures to be more representative of the third sector in Scotland and met more often to deal with issues in real time. Scotland Cares was set up as a centralised point for Scottish adults to sign up to volunteer, and emergency funding support was provided at pace and allocated in a more flexible way to support TSOs.

However, it is vitally important that the lessons learned during COVID-19 are reviewed to help embed good practice and new innovative ways of working; and to strengthen Scotland's third sector and volunteering.

5.5.1 Scotland's Volunteering Action Plan

The 'Road to Recovery' (Volunteer Scotland, 2022) report is timely as its findings will help inform the roll-out and ongoing development of the new ten-year Volunteering Action Plan for Scotland which aims to operationalise the Scottish Government 'Volunteering for All National Framework' (Scottish Government, 2022d). To help this process of 'evidence into action' three aspects should be addressed. First, that Volunteer Scotland's interpretation of the evidence is stress-tested and, where appropriate, developed further. Second, that there is a structured programme of dissemination and knowledge exchange events to engage relevant stakeholders as part of an ongoing development process. Third, that there should be an ongoing review of evidence on volunteering participation and community engagement to inform our understanding and learning about the long-term impact of COVID-19 on Scotland's third sector and volunteering. It is recommended that this work is integrated as part of the rollout of 'Scotland's Volunteering Action Plan'.

SIX

Wales

James Lundie, Sally Rees and Rhys Dafydd Jones

Image 6.1: Clwb Rygbi Nant Conwy

Note: 2020 saw the development of a rapid response support network in rural Conwy, including distributing shopping, prescriptions and meals as well as befriending

6.1 Introduction

We frame our chapter as a response to the pandemic, acknowledging the agency of volunteers and coordinators in unprecedented circumstances. This response was seen as exceptional for both informal and formal forms of volunteering. Informal, hyper-local associations often 'popped up', particularly during the first lockdown in spring 2020, facilitated by social media, while more formal organisations adapted their practices and focus to mobilise to support pandemic efforts (Boelman, 2021). However, to suggest that the voluntary sector in Wales is without issues is a misconception. In acknowledging the remarkable response and the broader reliance on voluntary activity, we also highlight its precarious condition through longer-term structural challenges of austerity and funding arrangements. We also highlight the divergent responses in Wales, with very different outcomes for organisations and volunteers.

The data discussed in this chapter were collected from two methods. First, a survey was conducted between April and June 2021 to understand the experiences of infrastructure organisations, such as County Voluntary Councils (CVCs), local authorities (LAs) and voluntary and community organisations (VCOs). The survey was designed to avoid duplication of other surveys undertaken in Wales around the same time, as well as enabling comparison with the other UK nations taking part in the study. The recommendations made in the Welsh Parliament report, 'Impact of COVID-19 on the voluntary sector' (Welsh Parliament Equality, Local Government, and Communities Committee, 2021) were also used to provide a framework for the survey. Most of the questions allowed for open-ended responses, which were then coded and analysed qualitatively with the aid of NVivo software. The survey was available in English and in Welsh. Sixty-four responses were received. Second, five semi-structured interviews were conducted with key stakeholders in August and September 2021. These stakeholders were involved in CVCs or LAs across Wales. They were invited due to their in-depth knowledge of voluntary sector infrastructure and delivery in Wales and asked to reflect on their experiences from March 2020. Interviews were conducted via Zoom: virtual fieldwork had been planned due to COVID-19 restrictions. The interviews were transcribed professionally and coded with NVivo software.

We begin by discussing the voluntary sector landscape in Wales in early 2020. We acknowledge the sector's ability to support a great deal of activity while faced by substantial economic challenges. We then proceed to focus on the response of the voluntary sector in Wales to the pandemic. We illustrate the different responses to COVID-19, which show that the growth in volunteering was not a universal experience. Building on these experiences, we reflect in the fourth section on the lessons to be learned from the pandemic. More 'blended' activities incorporating increased online presence, the inclusion of the voluntary sector in emergency planning, returning and new volunteers, and more sustainable funding appear as key issues. We conclude by outlining voluntary mobilisation; the diverse volunteering profile, and the challenges of ensuring that there is a cohesive response to emergency planning for the sector in crisis situations in the future.

6.2 The sector in 2020

Wales Council for Voluntary Action's (WCVA) submission to a Welsh Parliament call for evidence, 2020, provided a range of quantitative data, outlining that there were some 32,000 voluntary organisations in Wales in the years leading up to the pandemic: 7,300 of these were charities. 938,000 volunteers were estimated to contribute 145,000,000 hours/year in voluntary action, worth £1.7 billion, around 3.1% of Wales' Gross Domestic Product (WCVA, 2020, p 3). However, these contributions are not limited to financial value; volunteers also provide broader societal benefits that are less easily quantified, including 'individual wellbeing, social cohesion, inclusion, economic regeneration, and the development of social capital' (WCVA, 2020, p 3).

Those 7,300 charities typically reported lower turnover than in other parts of Great Britain. Fifty-three per cent were classified as 'micro-charities', with an annual turnover of less than £10,000: the largest share in Great Britain. Another 32 per cent were 'small charities', with an annual turnover of less than £100,000. Charitable income per head at just under £400 in Wales is half of the level in England or Scotland, at around £800. However, many larger, UK-wide charities operating in Wales are usually registered outside Wales, leading to some under-counting (WCVA, 2020, p 2).

There is a need to avoid projecting an image of the years preceding 2020 as stable. The voluntary sector in Wales was already in a precarious situation due to austerity, competitive tendering arrangements, shorter funding periods, and the unfolding, uncertain impacts of Brexit. Before we move to discuss these challenges, however, we outline the relationship between Welsh Government and the voluntary sector in Wales.

6.2.1 Structures

The relationship between the Welsh Government and the voluntary sector is often described as unique due to the constitutional obligation placed on the executive. Section 74 of the Government of Wales Act 2006 'requires Welsh Ministers to make a scheme setting out how they propose, in the exercise of their functions, to promote the interests of relevant voluntary organisations' (Welsh Government, 2014, p 3). This is the Third Sector Scheme and is operationalised as the Third Sector Partnership Council (TSPC), which is the Welsh Government's 'primary mechanism for engagement with the Third Sector' (Welsh Government, 2014, p 13). WCVA facilitate members' elections, with a view to reflect the voluntary sector's broad range of interests and activities.

The partnership was seen as valuable in fostering connections between the sector, government, and other bodies (Welsh Parliament Equality, Local Government, and Communities Committee, 2021).

The Welsh Government briefing, the *Third Sector Scheme* (2014) outlines the value of the voluntary sector to 'the long term economic, social and environmental well-being of Wales, its people and communities' (Welsh Government, 2014, p 8) in a context of austerity. While emphasising its legislative and policy primacy, it notes the value of 'volunteering as an important expression of citizenship and as an essential component of democracy' (Welsh Government, 2014, p 17). This more organic, subsidiarity approach evident in Wales is contrasted with the more 'top-down' approach experienced in England over the last decade (WISERD, 2020).

6.2.2 Challenges

Several challenges faced the voluntary sector in Wales prior to 2020. First, funding presented considerable multifaceted challenges. Austerity policies meant a reduction in public funds available. Government funding for the voluntary sector decreased from 55 per cent of its income in 2010–11 to 46 per cent in 2015–16, with Welsh Government grant funding declining from £350 million in 2010–11 to £257 million in 2016–17 (WCVA, 2019, p 3). Similarly, Welsh Government contract funding has reduced from £71.5 million in 2014–15 to £42.5 million in 2016–17 (WCVA, 2019, p 3). While legacy funding increased in this period, from £11.2 million in 2010–11 to £26.5 million in 2015–16, this only accounted for a small increase from 1 per cent to 2 per cent. The decline in public funding was met with an increase in public giving, from £295 million in 2010–11 to £416 million in 2015–16, accounting for 35 per cent of charities' income (WCVA, 2019, p 9). VCOs also moved towards more revenue-generating activities, such as training and room-hire (WISERD, 2020, p 3): activities which were severely impacted by the pandemic. While funding opportunities have reduced, operating costs have not fallen: indeed, many costs, such as fuel, have increased. Many charities in Wales were in a vulnerable position related to absorbing these costs: 'The Centre for Social Justice estimates that 24% of charities with an income of less than £1m have NO reserves, making their ability to survive and adapt during this time less likely' (WCVA, 2020, p 6, original emphasis).

Second, the nature and structure of funding created problems: 'Inadequate funding was an issue for many third sector and community groups going into the crisis' (WISERD, 2020, p 3). More project-focused and competitive tendering processes and shorter-term funding periods were viewed as focusing too much on specific, narrow targets and less on local needs and the broader societal benefits of services or projects. These approaches were also seen as creating competition rather than collaboration between organisations (WISERD, 2020). Similarly, a focus on short-term funding was critiqued as 'undermining organisational stability, for example due to high levels of staff turnover, limiting the ability to undertake forward planning, and placing constraints on joint working with potential partners across sectors' (WISERD, 2020, p 1). Many organisations spoke about a 'patchwork' approach to funding, drawing from several small pots. While this provided some resilience, it also challenged stability: 'the loss of one small pot of funding can have a disproportionately large impact on the overall project, since the cost of insurance and fuel etc. does not fall in equal proportion to the size of the funding' (WISERD, 2020, p 3). The reporting process was also considered prohibitively bureaucratic: 'many funding opportunities feature reporting requirements so time-consuming that many small organisations cannot even consider bidding for them, given their stretched capacity' (WCVA, 2019, p 6).

Third, the uncertainty around Brexit represented a challenge for the voluntary sector in the late 2010s. Alongside the loss of EU funding streams, uncertainty around the nature of any deal and a timeline for its implementation, and the nature of any replacement initiatives lasted for several years: 'Concerns remain about how EU funding may be replaced, with a lack of clarity around of its proposed successor, the UK Shared Prosperity Fund' (WCVA, 2019, p 7).

Finally, many UK-wide charities did not have structures which reflected the devolution arrangements in the UK. While Chaney and Williams (2003) report that organisations had begun to revise their structures to include a specific Welsh dimension in the early years of devolution, many Wales-specific roles had been reduced in the intervening years, often amalgamated into one role with responsibilities for all the devolved nations. This restructuring occurred as more powers were devolved, and frequently in organisations working in devolved fields, such as health, education and housing. As the Welsh Parliament's Equality, Local Government, and Communities Committee note, 'a lack of a Welsh expertise will affect the sector's ability to contribute to policy development as well as ensuring such policy is co-produced' (2021, p 13).

Having outlined the fragile position of the voluntary sector in Wales prior to 2020, we move now to consider the response of the sector during the pandemic.

6.3 The sector in the pandemic

Little did we think at the time of lockdown in late March 2020 that at the time of writing in February 2022 we would be continuing to live with the challenges of the pandemic. Indeed, we should take care not to homogenise the pandemic as one constant experience. New waves of infection and new strains of the virus emerge, lockdowns become shorter or more locally focused, COVID-19 passes are introduced, frequent testing is encouraged; masks are worn, hands are sanitised, vaccines are given; schools and universities return to teach in-person, and social distancing arrangements lead to a 'new normal'. Some changes have been gradual and may be temporary measures;

others may persist. As rates reduced and increased over time, restrictions were loosened and tightened. While we talk of one pandemic, it has many dimensions. Table 6.1 seeks to capture how voluntary action changed in Wales between March 2020 and June 2021.

Drawn from survey responses of VCOs and CVCs, the table highlights a range of experiences of the pandemic in Wales. The prominent narrative of voluntary participation during the pandemic suggests that many existing volunteers, who are often older people, shielded following government advice. This trend was met with more people volunteering, many of whom were furloughed, bringing a younger and more diverse profile to volunteering. As the infection rate reduced and furlough came to an end, these new volunteers returned to work. However, our research identifies more complexities, which we explore in this section. We follow six organisations to understand the different ways voluntary action changed through phases of the pandemic. Exploring these experiences from the ground up is useful in understanding how challenges are experienced and responded to differently.

6.3.1 U-shaped response

The first response is termed a U-shaped response, as it has a steep decline and a longer period of limited activity. This response is exemplified by survey response (011), a VCO in Neath-Port Talbot, a relatively deprived industrial area with a significant semi-rural hinterland. The VCO is specifically involved with an industrial heritage site. During the first lockdown of spring 2020, there was "no action on site". As restrictions began to be lifted in the summer of 2020, there was some volunteering on site: "The number of volunteers stayed the same and maintained the monument – grass cutting etc." (Respondent 011, survey). The profile of volunteers was bimodal: four teenage men and a mixed-gender group of six over-60s. Voluntary action was largely limited to the maintenance of the site, which continued during the autumn of 2020, including a period when local restrictions, which effectively prohibited entering the local authority area for non-essential reasons, were applied to Neath-Port Talbot, as well as the national 'firebreak' between 23 October and 9 November 2020. The respondent also highlights some diversity of the volunteer pool at this stage in terms of age and gender, but also homogeneity in terms of race.

A second national lockdown in Wales took place between 20 December 2020 and 12 March 2021, with "no action on site" during this period (Respondent 011, survey). This inactivity may be due to the minimal ground maintenance required during winter months, but it is also notable that no forms of action, such as a focus on online activities or diverting focus, took place. Finally, as the second lockdown ended on 13 March some restoration work took place: "work was carried [out] only by the Trustees mid-week and only in small numbers … a couple of weeks ago – beginning of May [a] complete team of volunteers met" (Respondent 011, survey). The complete team of volunteers meeting shows a steep return to pre-pandemic volunteering levels, completing the 'U' shape.

This example is useful to understand the specific experiences of volunteer activities in a particular post-industrial area, as well as forms of activity tied to site-specific participation. Such sites may be particularly important for localities, possibly serving as hubs of social activity or conveying a sense of place important for local communities. Such site-specific activities may also be related to individuals' wellbeing. In the case of industrial heritage sites, volunteers or their family members may have worked there. However, there is no suggestion here that volunteer efforts were directed towards other forms of action related to the pandemic effort.

6.3.2 Online shift

The second vignette is from an organisation (012) supporting carers. During the first lockdown, efforts were made to look

Table 6.1: Different typologies of voluntary activity during the pandemic in Wales

Type	First lockdown (March 2020 – 31 May 2020)	'Stay local' 1 and lifting of restrictions (1 June 2020 – 7 September 2020)	Local lockdowns and firebreak (8 September 2020 – 19 December 2020)	Lockdown 2 (20 December 2020 – 12 March 2021)	'Stay local' 2 and beyond (from 13 March 2021)
Prominent narrative	Decline in existing volunteers, but growth in new volunteers. Move online. Befriending activities.	Decline in volunteers as furlough ends, with previous volunteers continuing to shield.	Further decline in number of volunteers, although more activities resume 'in-person'.	Voluntary action focused on vaccine roll-out.	Focus on vaccine roll-out continues, but assumption of declining need for support.
'U-shape'	Decline in existing volunteers; restrictions limit new volunteers. Limited online action.	Limited volunteers in a socially distanced setting.	Some stability in volunteer numbers. Local restrictions may affect activities.	A further decline in volunteers.	Return of some volunteers and new volunteers.

Table 6.1: Different typologies of voluntary activity during the pandemic in Wales (continued)

Type	First lockdown (March 2020 – 31 May 2020)	'Stay local' 1 and lifting of restrictions (1 June 2020 – 7 September 2020)	Local lockdowns and firebreak (8 September 2020 – 19 December 2020)	Lockdown 2 (20 December 2020 – 12 March 2021)	'Stay local' 2 and beyond (from 13 March 2021)
Online shift	Move online, with regular support sessions.	Continuing online presence. Asking volunteers to focus on organisations' activities.	Some interest in volunteering, but doesn't translate into new numbers. Rolling back online support sessions.	Group reflects on outreach activities. Planning more online activities.	Considerable interest in volunteering, but again doesn't translate into new numbers. Embedding online activities into practice.
Stagnation and decline	Reduction in numbers due to social distancing. Closing. Move towards online activities.	New volunteers, revising practice. Remains closed.	Volunteer numbers decline. Remains closed.	Further decline in volunteer numbers. Remains closed.	Steady volunteer numbers, but lower than pre-pandemic. Remains closed. Exhausted members and volunteers.

after the wellbeing of volunteers through an online support group. The group realised that "the volunteers were all feeling helpless but at the same time were struggling with the situation so we started an online weekly support group for them to come along and talk to us about their fears" (Respondent 012, survey). Only "an average of 10 people who came along each week out of our bank of 140 volunteers" (Respondent 012, survey) but these continued through the pandemic. The group was proactive in reaching out to those didn't attend through personal calls. The support group continued after restrictions were eased during the summer of 2020, but by autumn the demand had reduced, and its frequency rolled back, meeting "twice a month instead of every week as it was not a good use of staff time to be online for two hours with only three people" (Respondent 012, survey). The group took the step of asking "all our volunteers not to go out into the community to do any volunteering and we adapted our roles so that they could use their experience and skills to carry on their volunteering role online" (Respondent 012, survey). Thus, the group sought to retain their volunteer pool, but with a refined online focus. By autumn, the group reported considerable interest from new volunteers:

'We had a lot of enquiries about online volunteering, however the success rate was two out of every ten and they were not totally committed to the volunteering role as the restrictions came and went and the messages were confusing, so we found that we were very quiet around this time.' (Respondent 012, survey)

The challenges in recruiting volunteers continued into the spring of 2021: "We had over 26 enquiries for volunteering in this period so far and only three have come forward with enthusiasm" (Respondent 031, survey). This experience contrasts with the experience of one CVC in southern Wales (031), that there are more volunteers than opportunities: "Priority is being given to existing volunteers so there is still a shortage of volunteering opportunities. Some volunteers are still too nervous to undertake activities in the community so they are choosing to do roles that can be done from home" (Respondent 031, survey). The prominent narrative often overlooks the mobilisation and sustenance of voluntary action after the initial end of furlough in 2020. Some fields, particularly those less directly focused on health and wellbeing, often faced continued restrictions or had difficulties in adapting for social distancing and took longer to return to being open to volunteers. Consequently, there are situations where people may have been, or are continued to be, denied volunteering opportunities. These differences suggest significant geographical or sectoral differences in returning to accept volunteers.

The winter lockdown of 2020–1 was a "very quiet time" and saw a change of emphasis to "concentrate more on how we could reach out to carers in the community online rather than the volunteering side" (Respondent 012, survey). By the spring of 2021, the group had consolidated its online presence, reviewing its activities with it: "We have had more time in the last few months to make changes to the way volunteers are inducted, how we can make the roles interesting but safe and how we can reach out to and support the volunteers" (Respondent 012, survey). As we discuss in the next section, more integrated use of online activity appears as an important issue for VCOs' future practice.

6.3.3 Decline

Three organisations spoke about a decline in voluntary activities during the pandemic. We turn to each of these in turn. First (013), a food bank in Neath-Port Talbot reported a decline at the outset of the first lockdown as the premises closed. A core of five volunteers maintained activities during this time, but could not be in the building at the same time. Easing of lockdown saw an increase in volunteers, with some new approaches to collect donations: "Our volunteers increased during this time and we introduced new roles for volunteers to collect from local donation points" (Respondent 013, survey). However, volunteer numbers declined during the autumn and winter when restrictions were tightened. As they loosened with the spring of 2021, there was little optimism that the organisation would see pre-pandemic volunteer levels: "The number of volunteers is still the same as lockdown 2 as some are still not confident to return to our setting" (Respondent 013, survey). While the initial reduction of restrictions in early summer 2020 brought some optimism, further restrictions and a decline in volunteers led to a more pessimistic account.

Second (026), a VCO focusing on mental health and wellbeing and operating throughout Wales gave a very concise account: "The workplace closed in March 2020 and is still closed." The organisation would have been closed for a period of 14–16 months when the survey was completed. Restrictions meant that the site initially had to close. For whatever reason, the organisation did not move services online. The site remained closed and no voluntary activities took place during the periods when restrictions were lifted and the infection rate was lower. Consequently, there is a question as to whether volunteering will ever resume, and in what form.

Finally (037), a VCO focusing on women's welfare, reported how they operated throughout the pandemic. Initially, the group didn't see a significant impact on their activities: the only significant change was pausing in-person support groups from March 2020. However, by early summer of 2021, the organisation reflected that:

> 'We have noticed that there is general fatigue among our members and volunteers. It has become more challenging to get them involved in activities due to worsening health conditions and life pressures as a result of the pandemic, including expectation to participate from

external stakeholders/agencies, like Welsh Government.'
(Respondent 037, survey)

There are several points to note here. First, is that while
many organisations reduced or paused activities, others
continued. As the comment about pressure to engage with
external bodies illustrates, some VCOs and their volunteers
may be as busy, if not busier than ever, without the time-
spaces to switch off and decompress. Second, the specific
work undertaken by the organisation often meant volunteers
and members reliving past trauma or engaging in distressing
situations: "Just because these meetings have moved online
and therefore don't have travel expenses, our volunteers
are regularly reliving their trauma for the benefit of public
bodies and their work going forward, and they should be
compensated for that" (Respondent 037, survey). The lack of
in-person support groups may also have accentuated wellbeing
issues for volunteers. Finally, the continued engagement with
online technology and working and volunteering from home
means that life balance can be compromised. Stacked online
activities, with a limited change of scene from a home context,
which itself might be distressing, can reduce morale.

Writing on women of colour's activism, Emejulu and Bassel
(2020) advance a politics of exhaustion. Exhaustion arises
from unsustainable practices, primarily through care work,
and taken as form of solidarity or emphasising collective needs
over that of the individual's wellbeing. For Emejulu and Bassel,
'extreme tiredness and demoralisation are both the signal that
activists are doing meaningful work, but also the breaking
point that stops them from containing with their activism
over the long term' (2020, p 401). Under the pressure of the
pandemic and its restrictions, and the longer-term strain of
austerity, as well as prejudice such as racism and misogyny,
it may be that key individuals for many organisations take a
decision to step back. Rather than a 'defeat', such decisions
emphasise self-care and can function as 'an endpoint and

gateway to withdrawal, but also a moment of reflection and rebirth' (2020, p 406).

Having outlined the diverse voluntary experiences during 2020–1, we now move to consider the lessons learned by the sector in Wales.

6.4 Looking forward

Four major themes emerge in thinking about lessons for the future from the voluntary sector response to the pandemic in Wales: more blended ways of working, incorporating online and offline activities; the involvement of the voluntary sector in emergency planning; strategies to encourage and sustain volunteering in the future; and funding for voluntary action. We consider each of these in turn.

6.4.1 Blended approaches

The pandemic and the subsequent restrictions saw more activities take place online. Some were new initiatives responding to the situation, such as online check-ins with members and volunteers to ensure their wellbeing. There were also many instances of already existing activities moving online, including training and induction, which had often been streamlined where appropriate to speed up volunteers' uptake of roles: "We adapted our system as quickly as possible, but it would have been good, on reflection, to offer more remote options for volunteering and volunteer induction, even before COVID-19 to make volunteering more accessible" (014, VCO, Monmouthshire). Organisations reflected on the potential for moving other activities online in the future, such as meetings: "We have also saved around £10,000 in travel expenses and will wherever appropriate, continue this [virtual media] way of working" (036, VCO, northern Wales). In this case, the potential for online meetings meant that time and money could be saved through not having to travel for relatively short meetings, and diverted elsewhere. It is important to note the potential significance in Wales, where there are relatively poor transport links within the country, particularly outside the M4/A48 corridor in the south and the A55 in the north.

However, digital ways of working present challenges. First, digital deprivation and the prevalence of broadband 'not-spots' in many parts of Wales, particularly rural western Wales, are well-known, and present barriers to participation. Second, physical presence in localities is particularly useful in helping give visibility to action, potentially recruit volunteers or raise awareness, and contribute to a sense of community. Many organisations noted that while more online presence, where appropriate, was a priority, it would not mean a wholesale abandonment of 'offline' activities. The closure of many community buildings over the last decade or so poses challenges for such approaches:

'[I]n a lot of instances, the focal buildings that people met all closed down … if communities don't have a focal of some kind, whether it be the school, whether it be the local church, chapel those are the types of things at a local level that actually still keep people gelled together.' (CVC officer, northern Wales, interviews)

Consequently, many organisations see the need to develop and embed blended approaches to volunteering to ensure opportunities and ways of working are accessible and inclusive.

6.4.2 Involvement in emergency planning

A second aspect reflected on by stakeholders was the involvement of the voluntary sector in emergency planning. A pattern emerged in the data, whereby areas affected by extreme weather events, such as flooding in Rhondda Cynon Taf and Conwy LAs in early 2020, had already brought together a range of emergency-focused bodies, while areas which hadn't been affected by extreme weather to the same degree seemingly took longer to make those connections and develop those relationships: "We know those community groups now. We know those volunteers now. We know those venues now. We didn't for Storm Dennis. We absolutely have nailed this now" (LA officer, south-eastern Wales, interviews).

Involvement of the voluntary sector in emergency planning was seen as useful in two ways. First, organisations can share their knowledge and expertise of their communities. Second, contact was made with a range of useful and related bodies that could be mobilised. One interviewee reflected that involvement would "help us develop their policies and their procedures with that voluntary and community aspect in mind, it would help us to put our own processes in place so that if we get the call we know exactly [what to do]" (CVC officer, mid Wales, interviews). For another respondent, involvement at a regional scale within south-eastern Wales was particularly helpful in bringing together relevant bodies around a 'mezzo-scale' that was neither too localised nor too broad.

Voluntary sector involvement ensured that important information was cascaded to relevant organisations. One respondent reflected on the value of having information available in an accessible, clear manner: "They just wanted to receive some information, such as safe volunteering, safeguarding. Just the basic information and up-to-date COVID-19 information. So they found us to be that trusted source of information for them" (CVC officer, mid Wales, interviews). Involving the voluntary sector in emergency planning thus allows an exchange of information that can be communicated, and the mobilisation of relevant voluntary groups.

6.4.3 Sustaining voluntary action

Respondents reflected on the challenges of sustaining voluntary participation in the future. As we noted in the third section, there is a general shortage of volunteer opportunities. Some organisations are, at the time of writing, still operating in a limited or scaled-back manner due to the pandemic; this more limited presence may continue after restrictions are lifted due to a lack of volunteers, including those previous volunteers who may continue to limit their social interaction. Others are prioritising returning or existing volunteers, potentially at the expense of younger volunteers:

> '[T]hose who volunteer as part of their college or university course may not be able to achieve the requested amount of volunteering hours, those that use volunteering as a stepping stone to employment may find that they struggle to get the appropriate experience they need for their career choice and those that use volunteering to get out of the house and make new friends could find themselves at home becoming isolated or lonely.' (Respondent 031, Local infrastructure organisation, Neath–Port Talbot, survey)

These young people may miss out on beginning their volunteering journeys as part of youth citizenship schemes (Mills, 2013), such as the Duke of Edinburgh's Award, or as part of a qualification. Indeed, opportunities for enrolling on such schemes were reduced during the pandemic (Boelman, 2021).

Yet, the mobilisation of volunteers in both formal and informal settings during the pandemic, and the appetite to volunteer, is something organisations wished to build on. Respondents reflected on the potential for workers, such as those who had volunteered at the outset of the pandemic, while furloughed or afforded more flexible home-working arrangements, to be given time off work for volunteering. Other respondents, however, wished to see more strategic contributions, reflecting on how workplaces could support voluntary action in a more sustained manner:

'Incentivise in a way that actually encourages more professional people to take up assisting the community sector with Trusteeships. Having that link as well into business where business could actually be they offer time as volunteering ... but offering that as a Trusteeship, rather than a bunch of staff going for a day to clear a woodland or something like that.' (CVC officer, south-western Wales, interviews)

While the commercialisation of VCOs, who are called to act more competitively to succeed in neoliberal and austere contexts, has been critiqued as moving the focus away from solidarity and support (Bassel and Emejulu, 2018), this is not to suggest that trustees are solely drawn from private enterprises, or adopt neoliberal mindsets. Rather, other experiences and transferable skills from their employees may be useful, as well as bringing back reflections to employers on their own practices, values and corporate responsibilities.

A final reflection is around removing the potential financial barriers to participation. In a study of young people involved in the National Citizenship Scheme, Mills and Waite (2018) note the challenges some people faced in being able to participate through 'hidden' costs. The impacts of COVID-19 on personal finance through job losses or the prospect of reduced work, as well as the sharp increase in the cost of living in early 2022 may bring further barriers to participation. One respondent reflected that covering volunteers' expenses would be helpful to remove this barrier, as well as giving recognition to volunteers for their efforts:

'[S]ometimes people think of volunteers as, oh unpaid. Don't need to worry about it. They'll just do it and I think we need to shift that mindset really, but volunteers will do it. Sometimes they just need a little bit of financial help to get them to where they need to be.' (CVC officer, mid Wales, interviews)

Highlighting this contribution would also further demonstrate the significance of voluntary activities for Welsh society, as these costs of volunteering would be more visible to policy-makers. As the interviewee reflected, the unwaged labour given is sometimes taken for granted. Reflecting on the skills brought by volunteers, as well as the value of their efforts and the costs borne by them would give more recognition to its value.

6.4.4 Funding

Finally, a significant issue identified by interviewees was around the sustainability of funding. Echoing points made in the second section, where projects are tendered on a competitive basis, smaller organisations feel that they lose out to larger organisations with more resources to target grant capture: "I don't think we should be put in the statutory pots so much, so that we've got to basically fight for a share of that pot. You know, very often our small organisations haven't got the time or the capacity to put funding bids together" (CVC officer, south-eastern Wales, interviews). Bassel and Emejulu (2018) note, however, that these larger organisations are less likely to tailor their needs to minority and marginalised groups, who can be further impacted by less prominent consideration of their requirements and input.

Shorter grant periods have also meant less time to build and consolidate relationships: "[E]verybody else is annually funded through grant. That can't be right. You can't build those trusting relationships that are required. We definitely need to have an influence over policy funding decisions and make then five years I think as a minimum" (LA officer, south-eastern Wales). Respondents identified longer grant periods and more collaboration between organisations as approaches that could contribute to more sustainable voluntary action.

6.5 Conclusion

We have recounted a range of responses to COVID-19 by voluntary organisations in Wales. The often-informal, hyper-local response, including 'pop-up' responses facilitated by social media, allowed immediate needs to be met in spring 2020. These mobilisations, often characterised as 'neighbourliness', filled a gap as organisations responded to the restrictions and reduction in volunteers who were shielding. The lockdown and furlough saw newer volunteers emerge, who contributed to a more diverse volunteer profile. However, there needs to be caution in heralding the pandemic as ushering in a new era of volunteering. As we have noted, different organisations operating in different fields report very distinct experiences in relation to volunteer opportunities. Some experienced a shortage of opportunities despite many ready volunteers. Other organisations reported a shortage of volunteers, or, even when there were volunteers, a sense of reluctance, leaving a volunteering gap.

Many responses also highlight fatigue. The pandemic brought new challenges and new approaches. Adapting practices to allow for social distancing, incorporating new online activities, or including new initiatives such as befriending, as well as a continuing or increasing demand meant that the voluntary sector had an even busier time than ever. Several organisations also had the impact of extreme weather events to deal with in February 2020 and January 2021, placing additional strain. However, these challenges exist atop long-standing challenges for the voluntary sector.

There are ongoing, longer-term structural issues facing the voluntary sector in Wales. A decade of austerity policies, competitive tendering processes, short-term grant cycles with more project-focused calls and the related reporting has created difficulties in planning, sustaining and focusing voluntary efforts. While there is little doubt that the Welsh Government recognises the value of the voluntary sector, and its approaches to fulfil its constitutional obligations are taken seriously through the TSPC, addressing concerns on funding would enable more sustainable practices that recognise voluntary activities' significance in Wales. This includes more strategic revisions around the nature of funding processes to longer-term, multi-year grant periods, as well removing barriers to volunteers, such as allowing volunteers to claim expenses. Broader policy discussions around work–life balance and social justice are also opportunities to consider volunteering's role in society.

Finally, more considerations could be given to integrating the voluntary sector into emergency planning. The agile response of the voluntary sector in meeting immediate needs at the outset of the pandemic, continuing its usual work alongside new initiatives, and mobilising to support the pandemic effort, such as the vaccine roll-out, demonstrates it value. While the next crisis may not be one around public health, evidence shows that areas that suffered flooding in early 2020 had established a solid working relationship between various actors, demonstrating the transferability of the voluntary effort during different kinds of emergencies. Where those partnerships already existed before the pandemic, information could be shared and volunteers mobilised more effectively.

SEVEN

The road(s) to recovery? Discussion and conclusion

Laura Crawford, Irene Hardill and Jurgen Grotz

Image 7.1: Embracing living with COVID-19

Note: This image was offered to the National Council of Voluntary Organisations by its member 'Home-Start Bolton' and today makes us reflect on 'embracing living with COVID-19'

7.1 Introduction

As we have seen in this book the impact of the COVID-19 pandemic on voluntary action across the UK has been profound. In this chapter, we draw some conclusions from the evidence presented in previous chapters, including the impact of the emergence of different relationships between voluntary action and the state across the four UK nations. We have employed this framework as a context for analysing the role of voluntary action in the pandemic and beyond, and thereby situate our analysis to help inform how we prepare for life beyond the pandemic.

The pandemic emergency legislation governing everyday life has followed different paths, but broadly the same trajectory, in each UK nation. The legislation changed on countless occasions, and, on the whole, in England was eased quicker than in the other nations, who were more cautious in reducing or removing restrictions throughout the pandemic, see for example Table 1.1 in Chapter One. Understanding and adhering to the many legislative changes since March 2020 has been a challenge for organisations mobilising voluntary action, staff have had to quickly understand the implications and then implement the necessary changes to practices to ensure that service delivery was compliant. The pandemic has been protracted, resulting in organisations constantly interpreting the rules and learning new ways to support voluntary action with enhanced safety measures in place. The very practice of volunteering, as a situated, embodied and emotional practice, is facing the need to adapt and change as organisations and volunteers prepare for life beyond the pandemic.

We started the research project in October 2020 with what turned out to be the flawed assumption that by the time we completed the research and wrote up our findings the pandemic would be behind us. We began writing this book in March 2022, two years after the team first met, virtually, to develop our research ideas. As we write the conclusion to this book in May 2022 restrictions on daily life across all four nations are being slowly removed, and statistics on infections and deaths are not reported daily, rather the news is dominated by the conflict in Ukraine and plight of the UK economy, a consequence of the pandemic, the Ukraine conflict and Brexit. In March 2022 the Scientific Advisory Group for Emergencies (SAGE) was stood down. This group was at the vanguard of the pandemic response, meeting regularly to provide scientific and technical advice to inform government decision-making throughout the pandemic. Commenting on this shift, Professor Carl Heneghan, Director of the Centre for Evidence-Based Medicine at the University of Oxford, remarked that: 'The standing down of SAGE signifies the end of the pandemic in the U.K. This is a remarkable turnabout of events given that just before Christmas, SAGE advisors were warning infections could hit two million per day and were pushing for further restrictions' (Knapton, 2022).

In April 2022 government funding was withdrawn from the ZOE COVID Study. In the ZOE study citizens self-reported COVID-19 symptoms using an app, leading to an enhanced understanding of the nature of the virus, infection levels, symptoms and geographical hotspots. By using 'near real-time data' from users, the app was able to predict potential outbreaks and was deemed 'an impressive demonstration of the power of citizen science' (ZOE COVID Study, 2020). Further to this, in April 2022 for much of the population free testing was suspended, with variations in eligibility and remaining testing infrastructure in each of the four jurisdictions (BBC, 2022). This major change in testing came just days before findings from Imperial College London and Ipsos MORI, covering 8 March to 31 March 2022, documented the highest recorded infection levels since the REACT-1 study started reporting cases in May 2020, with 6.37 per cent prevalence rates reported in England during this time period (UK Health Security Agency, 2022). For many, regular lateral flow testing was a sensible precaution to limit transmission undertaken before attending work or visiting others, now undermined by a lack of free lateral flow kits.

As these examples evidence, the infrastructures that supported broader public vigilance and awareness of the changing course of the pandemic are being dismantled, all while the virus continues to circulate. Although these significant changes may signal a shift from responding to an emergency to living with COVID-19, for many, the pandemic is far from over. For clinically vulnerable people who have shielded throughout the pandemic, the current climate is a time of heightened anxiety as all the measures that had contributed to a perceived sense of relative safety, for example, widespread mask-wearing, testing, reporting, no longer exist. While some people's lives may be back to pre-pandemic 'normal', the easing of restrictions is further entrenching the marginalisation of some groups, with real concerns about the long-term impact on those who have been socially isolated for prolonged periods of time. The tensions surrounding the transition to a 'new normal' across sectors are epitomised in the flight disruptions and cancellations experienced at UK airports over the Easter 2022 period. Passenger numbers increased as people sought to take advantage of the easing of travel restrictions, meanwhile airlines and airports were experiencing high-levels of COVID-19 related staff absences (Austin and Race, 2022).

Even though the pervasive impact of COVID-19 is no longer featuring so prominently in the public discourse, these broader changes directly impact the context within which voluntary action is operating. While many are eager to get on with their lives, and put the pandemic behind them, COVID-19 has exposed and exacerbated some of the deep-seated inequalities in UK society, leaving significant societal problems in its wake. Voluntary action is still responding to the pandemic and will continue to do so, even though the longer-term impacts of the virus are still not fully understood and recognised. As we noted in Chapter One, the pandemic was preceded by a period of significant social change for voluntary action, a period when important questions were raised about the role, position and contribution of voluntary action. These debates differed in each jurisdiction, and are reflected in variations in relations between the state and voluntary action (Woolvin et al, 2015). This book has demonstrated how the responses to COVID-19 were shaped by these relationships and the pandemic represents a critical moment for reflection, prompting renewed attention on the conditions that support voluntary action to flourish. In this final chapter we first briefly discuss the challenges of undertaking research in a pandemic; we then summarise the main impacts of the pandemic on voluntary action; and end by looking forward as we prepare for life beyond the pandemic.

7.2 Undertaking research in a pandemic

In 2020, the research community quickly mobilised to produce, share and disseminate knowledge on the impact of the pandemic at different spatial scales and in different organisational contexts. This included research commissioned by the various devolved administrations and research bodies, to understand the multifaceted responses across, within and between the public, private and voluntary sectors. In the UK, specialist networks and journals such as the Voluntary Sector Studies Network and *Voluntary Sector Review* consolidated and published research for a range of audiences. Research teams were formed, including ours, and a number were supported by funds from the Economic and Social Research Council (ESRC, 2021b).

In order to co-produce the research, we drew on the principles of Theory of Change (Weiss, 1972) to develop shared understandings of voluntary action, the research questions and a common approach to data gathering and analysis across the UK. This approach enabled the research teams to generate findings that would meet the needs of their jurisdiction but also allow for comparison across the nations.

The team's collective experiences of co-producing research during a pandemic provided new learnings on doing research in turbulent times. The ESRC Scheme provided appropriate resourcing to fund sector experts as co-researchers. The project outcomes were only possible because of this collaboration between academics and sector practitioners, and this funding played a pivotal role in facilitating the genuine partnership between our wider team. Funding dedicated towards a full-time project staff member was also critical to effective collaborative working. While each team member's contributions were funded on a fractional basis, each worked on the project at different days of the week around existing work pressures. The project staff member was a single point of contact, working as a central hub to draw together different work packages and support national teams to progress through their data collection around their existing commitments. The impact of funding clearly demonstrated how collaboration, much like some forms of volunteering, needs infrastructure and funding to support it.

'As in other areas of society, conducting research amid the COVID-19 pandemic requires adaptation' (Tremblay et al, 2021, p 1). Planning a research project, as we did, in the first lockdown of spring 2020 necessitated planning an entirely virtual programme of data collection to comply with emergency legislation and satisfy research ethics, both of the funder and our respective organisations and institutions. Online surveys and virtual interviews are certainly not new, but we faced an entire economy constrained by physical distancing rules. To ensure that we achieved reasonable response rates to surveys we needed both our practitioner co-investigators and practitioner Advisory Panel members to act as amplifiers, and sector 'gatekeeper' conduits. The role of the gatekeeper in facilitating research has been widely debated within the wider research community (Glynos and Speed, 2012; Yang et al, 2021), but in a pandemic, trusted sector gatekeepers were essential. Moreover, as we have already noted through the ESRC scheme we were able to apply for funding sector experts as co-investigators.

Even with these sector practitioners who had established relationships with the organisations they represented, the extreme pressures of responding to the pandemic impacted response rates, and made it difficult for some organisations to participate in our data collection. To enhance the impact of our study, we sought to disseminate our findings in real-time through our website, virtual events and social media. Sharing our emerging findings with organisations was a chance to give back to those who had given their time to our study. Various communication techniques were employed enabling the research to target diverse audiences. Some project communications were hosted via our project partners' websites, embedding our research within their normal round of activities, raising the profile of our project through these established networks. Creative outputs were also utilised such as blogs, podcasts and short think-pieces, providing snapshots of our findings in different formats. Moreover, virtual events were a chance to reach a broader audience, including those who perhaps didn't have time to complete a survey or participate in an interview. These events enriched our understanding of the most pressing issues facing organisations and addressed some of the gaps in knowledge from other data collection methods.

In addition to variable response rates, our data collection techniques captured distinct moments of the pandemic. Although the Be Collective and Team Kinetic data accounted for changes in volunteering over the course of the pandemic up to August 2021, and policy documents that pre-dated the pandemic were consulted, on the whole, we did not undertake a longitudinal study of the pandemic. The primary data gathered through the surveys and interviews in England, Wales and Northern Ireland were collected in spring/summer 2021. The timing of each survey is noteworthy as the participants' responses were indicative of the emergency legislation, infection levels, challenges and mood at that moment in time.

Furthermore, although research participants reflected on their work with volunteers, the voices of individual volunteers were not specifically sought in our study. Future work with a diverse range of volunteers, including those who stepped down during COVID-19, and those who volunteered for the first time, would be a fruitful line of enquiry. While our project achieved its objectives, it is important to recognise the limitations of our datasets and to interpret the findings as one study in a broader landscape of research activity.

We will now move to summarise the main contributions of our research and reflect on the legacy of the pandemic for voluntary action.

7.3 Key findings

Each national chapter offers a rich account of the data collected across the research, and while the results are broad and wide-reaching, we have grouped the key findings under the themes of volunteers, relationships, infrastructure and policy.

7.3.1 Volunteers

The advent of the pandemic drastically impacted everyday life for almost everyone. The result was an overnight radical change in all four nations to the demographics of who was volunteering, and who could volunteer. In this broader period of societal change, it is important to acknowledge the agency of citizens across the UK. Some people were moved to volunteer for the very first time, while others deepened their involvement with their communities. These responses were exceptional, as exceptional circumstances resulted in exceptional responses, by individuals, communities and organisations in every nation. A key finding of this study is that the willingness of citizens to help in times of crisis is widespread and strong, with little or no difference across the nations of the UK. Responses included spontaneous highly informal help, neighbourly help to non-kin, community-focused mutual aid, through to formal activities coordinated by voluntary and public sector organisations. Some private sector organisations pivoted to address unmet need, such as through the production of personal protective equipment required in hospitals and care homes (National Audit Office, 2020). The furlough scheme and increase in home working enabled some to volunteer, often for the first time; the absence of a daily commute freed up the time for many to support their local community. For others, the pandemic restrictions introduced new time pressures, especially for those home-schooling or with increased caring responsibilities.

Some groups were more likely than others to step back from volunteering, such as older people and those instructed to shield and restrict social contact beyond household members. Some volunteering moved online while other roles were impossible to facilitate in a digital format, leading to the pausing of certain volunteering opportunities. As observed across the chapters, the offers of volunteer support did not always neatly map onto demand, so many of those who stepped forward were not given roles or formal responsibilities. The long-term impact of this on enthusiasm to volunteer in the future remains to be seen. During the data collection repeated calls were made to invest in mechanisms to support organisations to translate offers of help into meaningful volunteering opportunities.

While the VCS has long considered the importance of making volunteering accessible to all, the pandemic has resulted in the creation of new barriers that have impacted who can, or who feels able to, engage in volunteering. Many long-standing volunteers who have shielded have lost confidence, prompting renewed attention on the importance of volunteer wellbeing, both for those actively involved, and those who have paused their engagement. Moreover, the all-encompassing nature of the pandemic has taken a physical and emotional toll on the sector, paid staff and the volunteers who support its work. As discussed in Chapter Six, for some, especially those volunteers with lived experience connected to the communities they support, temporary or permanent withdrawal from volunteering may be an act of self-care. Organisations are tasked with finding a balance between supporting those who wish to return, without pressuring those who are not yet ready to re-engage. This has included implementing measures such as additional training, and peer support schemes to provide volunteers with the tools to return to roles, develop new skills and adapt to new ways of working. Alongside re-engaging with long-established volunteers, organisations are also eager to sustain the involvement of those new volunteers by offering more flexible roles that could be managed alongside paid work commitments.

7.3.2 Relationships

During the pandemic, new relationships were built within and between organisations, sectors and communities, and existing relationships were strengthened. The research has evidenced how collaborative relationships were pivotal to the effective coordination of joined up responses, however, the crisis conditions also exposed areas where there is a lack of partnership working. During the first lockdown new partnerships developed quickly as formal volunteer involving organisations in the public and voluntary sector offered support and advice to mutual aid groups as they developed protocols for supporting and mobilising volunteers. Some responses, especially at the start of the pandemic in 2020, were quick, creative, often facilitated by social media and WhatsApp groups; but sometimes these interventions were short-lived, and not always suitably connected to existing systems and processes. The cessation of such activity must not immediately be deemed negative, as for some groups there was no desire to continue or to formalise into a more sustainable entity. However, the collaboration was indicative of the need for relationships to be nurtured, so in the event of future crises, various stakeholders have the necessary mechanisms and platforms through which to work collaboratively.

One of the changes that facilitated collaborative working during the pandemic was the shift in the traditional processes and practices employed for recruiting, training and supporting volunteers. In Scotland, for example, the National Voluntary Sector Coordination (NVC) Hub was set up to provide a centralised resource for any areas that needed prompt volunteer support over and above that provided through the existing structures. The NVC Hub provided volunteer support for the vaccination and testing programmes wherever sufficient volunteer support was not available, contributing over 50,000 hours. In other cases, processes were streamlined to facilitate faster onboarding of volunteers, although there were some concerns, especially around safeguarding. Looking forward, there is a need to review what bureaucratic processes and systems are essential, and where a more creative approach could be adopted to support the rapid mobilisation of voluntary action.

7.3.3 Infrastructure

A recurring theme in the preceding national chapters has been the impact of the pandemic on voluntary action in communities of place, where an uneven geography has emerged. In many cases, these local variations were indicative of the legacy of policy interventions and investment in community infrastructure. Some local communities with prior experience of responding to an emergency, such as those communities in Wales that were devastated by flooding in February 2020, were able to mobilise voluntary action better than others in the first lockdown. In these areas there were clear and established mechanisms that could be built on through Local Resilience Forums, along with legislative duties, and processes and procedures which govern how local areas should respond to emergencies. Sharing local knowledge and making connections with a range of bodies such as local authorities, the police, utilities companies, Welsh Government, Natural Resources Wales, the health board and first responders facilitated community resilience through local partnership working.

There is a large body of literature on the importance of community-led infrastructure and the critical role it played in supporting volunteering pre-pandemic (Davis Smith, 2019) and organisations including the Local Trust played a key role in supporting such research during the pandemic (Ellis Paine, 2020; Macmillan, 2020b). Some of the infrastructure organisations in place at the start of the pandemic were a legacy of investments made by organisations such as the Big Lottery Fund which, in the case of England, were not the result of current government policy.

In some locations, for example in parts of England, the infrastructure to support voluntary action had all but disappeared while in other areas there was still a healthy network. However, one prominent feature of the pandemic was the repurposing of existing infrastructure to support the emergency response. For example, in Gateshead, this involved local authority leisure and community centres pivoting to become physical spaces for the coordination of COVID-19 support.

While voluntary action in Northern Ireland is an important site for mixing across ethno-religious divisions, at the same time organisations, especially at local level, remain embedded in a single community identity (Acheson, 2011). As a result, in many cases organisations tend to rely on their 'own' community for support and volunteers. We found evidence, however, that under the pressure of the pandemic some of these fault lines fractured and cross-community working increased; we have no evidence on the extent to which these effects will last.

In Scotland, there was an established and effective working relationship between the Scottish Government and the third sector before the outbreak of COVID-19. This was underpinned by the co-produced National Volunteering Outcomes Framework, the network of 32 Third Sector

Interfaces (TSIs) and funding support for the sector. However, the impact of COVID-19 was to deepen and strengthen the relationships between infrastructure organisations, particularly at the local level, with the contribution of TSIs as centres of volunteering expertise being more widely recognised. This supported the immediate resilience response as well as the provision of longer-term support.

7.3.4 Policy

We now turn to examine the impact of political decisions and choices made before 2020, and how these have constrained or enabled voluntary action during the pandemic. In the years preceding 2020 the relationship between the state and sector should not be thought of as stable across all the four nations (Woolvin et al, 2015). Pre-pandemic, the devolved governments and the voluntary sector in Wales and Scotland retained a spirit of partnership working and an established relationship between, for example, the Third Sector Unit in Welsh Government and the Welsh national infrastructure body. As discussed in the previous section, the Scottish Government's Third Sector Unit already had strong relationships with key partners including Volunteer Scotland, the Scottish Council for Voluntary Organisations, the TSI Scotland Network and Impact Funding Partners. The recent history of Northern Ireland and the role of the voluntary sector in that history have been markedly different to the rest of the UK. Continuing political instability since the 1998 Good Friday Agreement has kept alive the idea of voluntary action as a legitimate source of social stability, even if at the same time it has left existing volunteering policy out of date. The experience of the pandemic shows the urgent need to address this. First to ensure that all those organisations most at risk from the disruption it caused to volunteering have the support they need; and second, that the role of volunteering is recognised in emergency planning and structures put in place to give that effect.

Our analysis in Chapter Two drew attention to the similarities and differences that became apparent across the four jurisdictions. The prevailing relations between voluntary organisations and the respective governments helped to not only shape the response to the pandemic, but also to enhance the relations themselves. The lack of government engagement in England meant the response was largely focused on public health guidance, whereas in Wales and Scotland, voluntary organisations were involved in the allocation and disbursement of state monies. In terms of the citizen response, this was largely similar across the four jurisdictions, and again was predominantly determined by the form and focus of the existing voluntary action opportunities pre-pandemic. In terms of voluntary sector organisations, again this was determined by what they were already involved with pre-pandemic, and what the prevailing civil society spaces enabled them to achieve in response to the pandemic. Some aspects of the social, political and policy spaces were similar in the four jurisdictions, whereas in other key areas they were markedly different. These differences impacted directly upon what citizens and organisations were able and unable to accomplish.

7.4 Looking forward

As the sector looks forward, organisations are reflecting on and learning lessons from the pandemic to achieve, as Volunteer Scotland (2022) highlights, a 'steady state'. But attaining a steady state is further complicated by the continuing demands placed on the voluntary sector, not least as a result of conflict in Ukraine and the cost of living crisis. As Charity Link (2022) articulate, 'just when we thought we might be able to breathe a sigh of relief and sift through the debris left by COVID-19 pandemic, here we are in national crisis again'. Previous research into volunteering during crises has illustrated that while volunteering in emergencies almost always occurs, there also almost always appears to be a lack of learning from such volunteer involvement (Aguirre et al, 2016). There is already anecdotal evidence emerging that this could be the case with COVID-19, as many organisations have found it difficult to 'resist the bureaucratic creep' and old ways of working (Cook et al, 2020, p 2).

The pandemic has had a profound and uneven impact on UK society, with the British Academy independent review considering the impact in three broad areas including health and wellbeing; communities, culture and belonging; and knowledge, employment and skills (British Academy, 2021). The report detailed the important role voluntary action played in supporting communities. Voluntary action is playing a very visible role in addressing societal need, particularly in areas exacerbated by the pandemic, such as mental health, and helping families cope with the rising cost of living.

When considering the legacy of COVID-19 on voluntary action, there are certainly positives to commend, and we can remain hopeful that these positives will impact future landscapes of volunteering. In particular, the value of volunteering has arguably received wider recognition than ever before, including informal volunteering and the work of mutual aid and hyper-local groups (Ellis Paine, 2020). Many public and voluntary sector organisations have found meaningful ways to support these groups, combining local and organisational knowledges to establish more equitable partnership working. The future is likely to involve the delivery of more 'blended' activities, offering volunteers and service users a chance to engage both digitally and face-to-face. However, there are significant challenges that remain, namely, how to support the inclusion of groups that have been marginalised from volunteering and are finding it difficult to re-engage.

7.4.1 Geography matters

The pandemic has also brought into sharper relief the ambiguities of devolution, including the different policy approaches in the four nations to non-reserved issues such as health and voluntary action. The pandemic did not respect borders! But the responses across the four nations to mitigate the effects of COVID-19 raised awareness of policy divergence and borders.

One theme that emerged particularly in Wales and Northern Ireland was the challenge of borders. Northern Ireland is the only part of the UK with a land border with another state. The border is open and in normal times tens of thousands of people cross it every day for work, family life and socialising. There is a long history of cooperation between Northern Ireland and the Republic of Ireland in delivering health care to border communities and some hospital specialisms are provided on an all-island basis. With the onset of the pandemic aligning regulations proved problematic, with the Northern Ireland Executive tending to follow the English lead rather than the much stricter regime enforced in Ireland. In particular, the 5km travel limit imposed in Ireland in the first lockdown effectively closed the border. Many of the pressures on volunteering were similar. Good working relations between Volunteer Now in Northern Ireland and Volunteer Ireland, the two voluntary sector infrastructure bodies, enabled the sharing of experience and mutual learning.

In Wales, three specific aspects related to borders were noted: divergence from England; activities crossing the Anglo-Welsh border; and internal borders. Divergence in policy-making from England was visible during the early summer of 2020, several videos of tourists from England visiting Wales while inadvertently breaking Welsh rules went viral, unaware that there were different regulations at work (BBC, 2020a), and locations, such as Chester City's football ground, where the border meant different regulations existed in close proximity, were discussed. Devolution is not a new phenomenon and having different regulations in Wales compared to England is not a novel experience. However, there was an issue of communication, and the lack of attention or reflection in

Anglocentric print media of the different situation in Wales. Unlike in Scotland or Northern Ireland, there are no Welsh versions of UK 'national' dailies. As the @ThatsDevolved Twitter account notes, many media articles discuss issues relating to England uncritically and without qualification, implying their universality, further confounded that in many fields the 'British Government' only has jurisdiction over England. This is a long-standing and broader issue, but the pandemic has highlighted the need for clearer communication.

Pandemic regulations restricted mobility, including the crossing of borders within and beyond each jurisdiction. Respondents based in north-eastern Wales, in particular, spoke about some difficulties in having different policies at work when many activities required crossing the border for work purposes and back again. These issues are not unique to Wales, with many countries having porous borders or different policies within due to federal or devolved arrangements. However, the lack of clarification, or seeming consideration, on what to do when basic arrangements, for example, attending a hospital appointment in England as a Welsh patient required crossing a border, caused some contestation in the region.

Cross-border activities are not limited to the Anglo-Welsh border: during the autumn of 2020, various local restrictions were in place, effectively limiting the crossing of local authority boundaries. The different restrictions in place at different times or relating to specific issues may be the cause of confusion here. However, clear and specific guidance could be given when voluntary activity involves crossing a border.

7.5 Conclusion

The pandemic has given us a better understanding of how and why voluntary action occurs. It introduced more people to volunteering, increased recognition of the role and value of voluntary action, and brought about more collaboration between individuals, organisations and communities. While we have long recognised that the propensity to volunteer changes over one's lifetime (Brodie et al, 2011; Hogg, 2016), there are signs that this temporal pattern is changing because of the pandemic.

People are motivated by need and a desire to help non-kin, but voluntary action needs to be supported to channel that help into positive action. That support could be guidance for those setting up mutual aid groups, volunteer matching infrastructure, and investment in onboarding and training. In some ways, the employment of digital technologies during the pandemic has changed how voluntary action is mobilised and practised. Embracing digital ways of working does present some challenges, including addressing digital deprivation and the prevalence of broadband 'not-spots' in many rural locations across the UK.

Finally, at the start of the pandemic, on 30 April 2020, Baroness Pitkeathley, President of the National Council for Voluntary Organisations, spoke of charities as part of the broader landscape of voluntary action, as: 'the eyes, ears and conscience of society: they mobilise, they provide, they inspire, they advocate and they unite' (Hansard, 2020, col 290), and although voluntary action has changed it remains very much 'who we are' and 'what we do' (Brewis et al, 2021). What we can say with some certainty is that the approaches to mobilising voluntary action in the four nations of the UK will be different and that any future research needs to recognise this. This study, and others funded by the ESRC as part of the UKRI COVID-19 call, have demonstrated the importance of offering collaborative cross-sectoral research funding and how researchers and voluntary organisations can work together to understand and improve the volunteer experience.

Glossary

Austerity Following the financial crisis in 2008 the UK government introduced an austerity programme of fiscal policies with ongoing reductions in public spending. This also led to reduced income for voluntary sector organisations.

Big Lottery The Big Lottery Fund, now called the National Lottery Community Fund, donates money from the National Lottery to good causes, including health, education, environment projects and community groups.

Big Society A political ideology that was a key component of David Cameron's Conservative Party agenda on their election as part of the Coalition Government in 2010. It was characterised by an integration of free market, small-state ideology, social solidarity and voluntarism. This policy applied to England. Its stated aim was to create a society that empowers people and communities. It was, rightly or wrongly, seen as a cover for austerity and cuts to public services, and was dropped prior to the 2015 General Election. Its two lasting legacies are the Localism Act 2011 and the National Citizen Service.

Blended, approaches or activities Ways of working, collaborating, including volunteering which incorporate online and face-to-face activities.

Charity Commission Northern Ireland The Charity Commission for Northern Ireland is the independent regulator of charities in Northern Ireland.

#CharitySoWhite A campaign which started in August 2019 as a Twitter hashtag and has developed into an organisation which seeks to address racism within the charity sector by encouraging candid and critical conversations about racism. The campaign has a vision of a charity sector that takes a lead on talking about and rooting out racism. It wants to see a shift in fundamental structures across the charity sector, where the sector, its leaders and decision-makers reflect the communities that they work with. Their website is https://charitysowhite.org

Civil Society Strategy This Strategy for England was outlined in a document by the Cabinet Office in London in 2018, called 'Civil Society Strategy: Building a future that works for everyone'. The strategy set out how government intended they work with and support civil society.

Co-production of knowledge In this book our team of academics and sector experts worked collaboratively applying principles of the co-production of knowledge. In this sense co-production recognises and foregrounds the use of different knowledges, not merely epistemic knowledge, but also techne and phronesis, the knowledge of practitioners and citizens, during the research process.

Community Community, like volunteering, is not a simple descriptive word but one with shifting and disputed meaning. Community is a complex and ambiguous term. It generally requires context such as geography, ethnicity or shared experience, interest or work practice. It can be contentious because membership of specific communities is neither fixed nor automatically agreed. People are likely to belong to multiple communities, whether these are geographical or of interest and/or shared experiences. Subjectively area, neighbourhood and community mean different things to different people at different times. Community like neighbourhood has re-emerged in both academic and policy circles in post-war Britain as an important setting for many of the processes that shape social identity and life chances.

Council for Voluntary Service – England In England Councils for Voluntary Service are one type of local voluntary sector infrastructure organisation, that exist to support frontline voluntary, community and social enterprise organisations.

County Voluntary Council (CVC) – Wales In Wales the local voluntary sector infrastructure organisations are called CVCs. Like other voluntary sector infrastructure organisations they provide advice and information to local voluntary and community groups on volunteering, funding sources and a wide range of other issues.

Department of Business, Energy and Industrial Strategy This is a ministerial department of the UK Government responsible for business, industrial strategy, science, research and innovation, energy and clean growth and climate change. Some of the Department's responsibilities have been devolved to the Northern Ireland Assembly, Scottish Government and the Welsh Government specifically relating to the economic development, the environment and climate change. However, other areas are not, such as UK Research and Innovation, which administers research funding across the seven Research Councils for the UK.

Department for Communities – Northern Ireland This is a department of the Northern Ireland Civil Service responsible for equality, anti-poverty, sports, arts and culture, languages, finding employment, historic environment, housing, regeneration, benefits and pensions, community and voluntary sector development, social legislation and child support.

Department for Digital, Culture, Media and Sport This is a ministerial department of the UK Government with priorities to grow the economy, connect the UK, encourage participation, sustain excellence and promote Britain, supporting the media and ensuring social responsibility. This Department has responsibility for volunteering and the voluntary sector for England. Volunteering and the voluntary sector are devolved to the Scottish Government, Welsh Government and Northern Ireland Assembly.

Discourse analysis In this study discourse analysis was used to analyse policy documents. Discourse analysis is a research method that is primarily interested in studying spoken or written language to analyse underlying meaning in relation to the broader social context in which it was produced.

Economic and Social Research Council (ESRC) The ESRC provides funding and support for research and postgraduate training for economic, social, behavioural and human data science. The ESRC was first established in 1965 as the Social Science Research Council and is part of UK Research and Innovation.

Firebreak A short period of lockdown and tighter restrictions designed to reduce COVID-19 transmission rates sharply.

Furlough Furlough is another term for 'The Coronavirus Job Retention Scheme'. This was a temporary scheme designed to support employers whose operations have been affected by COVID-19. It meant employees who could not work because of COVID-19 restrictions would continue to be paid.

Good Friday Agreement The Belfast or Good Friday Agreement was reached on 10 April 1998. It was an agreement between the British and Irish governments and most of the political parties in Northern Ireland on many of the issues which had caused the conflict. The agreement saw an end to the majority of violence and made provision for devolved, power sharing government in Northern Ireland.

GoodSam GoodSam is the global telephone app used for the NHS Volunteer Responder Scheme in England.

Gross Domestic Product (GDP) According to Organisation for Economic Co-operation and Development, GDP is the standard measure of the value added created through the production of goods and services in a country during a certain period.

Levelling Up Levelling Up describes a UK Government programme to spread opportunity more equally across the UK. The programme was presented to Parliament by the Secretary of State for Levelling Up, Housing and Communities in February 2022. Funding will be allocated to all parts of the UK as part of this programme.

Local Resilience Forums, Emergency Preparedness Groups and Resilience Partnerships These are multi-agency partnerships made up of representatives from local public services, including the emergency services, local authorities, the NHS, the Environment Agency and others. They aim to plan and prepare for localised incidents and catastrophic emergencies. They work to identify potential risks and produce emergency plans to either prevent or mitigate the impact of any incident on their local communities. In England and Wales they are referred to as Local Resilience Forums. In Scotland there are national, regional and local resilience partnerships, supplemented by voluntary sector resilience groups and a voluntary sector resilience partnership. In Northern Ireland they are referred to as Emergency Preparedness Groups.

Local Trust The Local Trust was established in 2012 to deliver Big Local, a National Lottery Community Fund funded programme across neighbourhoods in England. During the pandemic the Trust supported research on the impact of the pandemic. The Local Trust describe themselves as a 'place-based funder supporting communities to achieve their ambitions'. The Local Trust manages a scheme that is funded by the National Lottery Community Fund called Big Local. The Big Local scheme provides £1m to 150 communities in England, with a vision to produce 'empowered, resilient, dynamic, asset-rich communities'.

Lockdown This term was used during the pandemic to describe restrictions on people's movements. It included mandatory instructions such as 'stay-at-home' or 'stay local'.

Micro volunteering Micro volunteering is a contested term that has received renewed attention during the pandemic as it is considered to be one way to reduce barriers to volunteering for working-age adults. A good definition is offered by Browne et al (2013): 'Micro-volunteering is bite-size volunteering with no commitment to repeat and with minimum formality, involving short and specific actions that are quick to start and complete.'

Mutual aid Mutual aid is a term that has been used for a long time and has many meanings. Its origins lie in anarchist theory, but it was also later used to describe parts of voluntary action and more recently to describe self-help groups in health and social care. During the pandemic the term was frequently used to describe unpaid help through informal groups set up by people to support and help others in their local community, often using online groups.

National Council for Voluntary Organisations (NCVO) NCVO is the national membership organisation for voluntary organisations in England.

NHS Volunteer Responders Programme – England The NHS Volunteer Responders Programme is a partnership between NHS England and NHS Improvement, GoodSAM and the Royal Voluntary Service. It was originally established to support people who were asked to shield due to underlying health conditions. The programme aimed to match local volunteers with individuals or organisations such as pharmacies through the GoodSAM app.

Office of the Scottish Charity Regulator The Scottish Charity Regulator is a non-ministerial department of the Scottish Government with responsibility for the regulation of charities in Scotland.

Research ethics Consideration of research ethics is a requirement for all research undertaken by UK universities. Researchers must ensure that all people taking part in research should only do so if they have given their fully informed consent. It also requires that all procedures planned and carried out in any research study have to be independently reviewed to ensure that they are ethical.

Royal Voluntary Service (RVS) RVS is a charity (1015988 in England and Wales and SC038924 in Scotland), to deliver practical support 'through the power of volunteering'.

Scottish Council for Voluntary Organisations (SCVO) SCVO is the national membership organisation for voluntary organisations in Scotland.

Scottish Household Survey (SHS) The SHS is an annual, cross-sectional survey on the composition, characteristics, attitudes and behaviour of private households and individuals as well as evidence on the physical condition of Scotland's homes.

Shielding The term shielding was used to describe how to protect those citizens at highest risk of severe illness if they caught COVID-19. Government guidance was given, which included minimising social interaction.

Third sector Third sector is a term often linked to the New Labour years in England when it was popularised. It is often used interchangeably with voluntary, community and social enterprise sector or voluntary and community sector.

Third Sector Interfaces (TSIs) – Scotland TSIs provide a single point of access for support and advice for the third sector within local areas. There is a TSI in each local authority area in Scotland (see also 'voluntary sector infrastructure organisation').

Third sector organisation (TSO) This term usually describes any organisation, whether or not incorporated, that operates for a social purpose. It generally includes charities; a wide range of enterprises operating for primarily social purposes, including co-operatives or community interest companies; and all forms of unincorporated associations.

Third Sector Partnership Council – Wales In Wales the Third Sector Partnership Council is chaired by the Minister responsible for the Third Sector Scheme and is made up of representatives of third sector networks working across 25 areas of third sector activity along with the Chief Executive Officer of Wales Council Voluntary Action. The Third Sector Partnership Council considers issues that relate to the strategic objectives and functions of the Welsh Government and which engage the interests of the Third Sector, and makes recommendations to the Welsh Government.

TSI Scotland Network TSI Scotland Network is the network of 32 TSIs across Scotland and is supported to carry out its main functions by the Third Sector Unit of Scottish Government.

UK Research and Innovation (UKRI) UKRI was formed in 2018 and is a non-departmental public body sponsored by the Department of Business, Energy and Industrial Strategy.

Vision for Volunteering – England Vision for Volunteering is a ten-year initiative outlining a vision for volunteering in England. Driven by a steering group of more than 20 organisations with contributions from over 350 people, the Vision aims to build a clear, ambitious and achievable ten-year plan to improve volunteering with measurable actions.

Voluntary action Voluntary action is difficult to define, and has varying interpretations in different geographical and organisational contexts. For this book we used the following definition: 'Voluntary Action is the commitment of time and energy, for the benefit of society and the community, the environment or individuals outside, or in addition, to one's immediate family. It is undertaken freely and by choice, without concern for financial gain. It comprises the widest spectrum of activity for example, community development, arts, sport, faith based, education, neighbourliness, youth, environmental, health and direct care. This can include activities undertaken through public, private and voluntary organisations as well as community participation and social action in associations and groups which may not be registered or don't have a confirmed structure' (Grotz, 2021, p 9).

Voluntary and community organisation This term usually describes any organisation, whether or not incorporated, that operates for a social purpose. It generally includes charities; a wide range of enterprises operating for primarily social purposes, including co-operatives or community interest companies; and all forms of unincorporated associations.

Voluntary and community sector (VCS) This term, often used interchangeably with 'third sector' or 'voluntary, community and social enterprise sector', has no clearly agreed definition. It usually describes any organisation, whether or not incorporated, that operates for a social purpose. It generally includes charities; a wide range of enterprises operating for primarily social purposes, including co-operatives or community interest companies; and all forms of unincorporated associations.

Voluntary and Community Sector Emergencies Partnership – England In England, the Voluntary and Community Sector Emergencies Partnership is a partnership of local and national voluntary and community sector organisations, hosted by the British Red Cross, providing space and opportunity for local and national voluntary and community organisations to come together.

Voluntary, community and social enterprise sector This term, often used interchangeably with 'third sector' or 'voluntary and community sector', has no clearly agreed definition. It usually describes any organisation, whether or not incorporated, that operates for a social purpose. It generally includes charities; a wide range of enterprises operating for primarily social purposes, including co-operatives or community interest companies; and all forms of unincorporated associations.

Voluntary sector infrastructure organisations Voluntary sector infrastructure organisations support with advocacy, partnerships and volunteering. The term is used differently in the nations of the UK, see for example Council for Voluntary Service in England; County Voluntary Council in Wales; with a wider range in Northern Ireland including Volunteer Bureaus and Volunteer Centres. In Scotland the term describes a variety of organisations supporting or coordinating volunteering (see definition in Chapter Five for Scotland).

Voluntary Sector Resilience Partnership See 'Local Resilience Forums, Emergency Preparedness Groups, and Resilience Partnerships'.

Volunteer, volunteering Volunteering encompasses activities undertaken by choice, without concern for financial gain that benefits non-kin. Not everyone is likely to call such activities 'volunteering', therefore in the Community Life Survey in England, respondents are asked if they have provided unpaid help through groups, clubs and organisations (see volunteering, formal). The Community Life Survey also identifies 'informal volunteering' by asking about any unpaid help an individual may have given to other people, such as a neighbour, but not a relative, and not through a group, club or organisation. As the way people speak about volunteering varies greatly, it is very important to clarify what people mean when they use the term.

Volunteer involving organisation (VIO) VIO describes any organisations which involves volunteers, which can be in the voluntary, public or private sector. VIOs may involve volunteers in their own activities or match volunteers with volunteering opportunities in other organisations.

Volunteer Now Volunteer Now is a charity (NI 602399) to promote and support volunteering across Northern Ireland.

Volunteer Scotland Volunteer Scotland is a charity (SC013740) to encourage, stimulate and support volunteering principally in Scotland.

Volunteering, formal This term is used to distinguish volunteering through any groups, clubs or organisations from other forms of volunteering. It is often used in surveys but does not include clear definitions of 'formal'. Formal volunteering is often associated with specific volunteer roles, set hours and may involve forms of supervision.

Volunteering, informal This term is used to distinguish volunteering that is not delivered through or organised by groups, clubs or organisations. It is often used in surveys but does not include clear definitions of 'informal'. It can include helping neighbours or participating in social action.

Wales Council for Voluntary Action (WCVA) WCVA is a national membership organisation for voluntary organisations in Wales.

References

Acheson, N. (2010) 'Welfare state reform, compacts and restructuring relations between the state and the voluntary sector: Reflections on Northern Ireland's experience', *Voluntary Sector Review: An International Journal of Third Sector Research, Policy and Practice*, 1(2): 175–192.

Acheson, N. (2011) 'A case of avoiding "political mumbo jumbo": Do collective identities within ethnically diverse voluntary associations spill over to other contexts? Reflections on Northern Ireland experience', *Policy & Politics*, 39(2): 203–220.

Acheson, N., Harvey, B., Kearney, J. and Williamson A.P. (2004) *Two Paths, One Purpose: Voluntary Action in Ireland, North and South*, Dublin: Institute for Public Administration.

Aguirre, B.E., Macias-Medrano, J., Batista-Silva, J.L., Chikoto, G.L., Jett, Q.R. and Jones-Lungo, K. (2016) 'Spontaneous volunteering in emergencies', in D.H. Smith, R.A. Stebbins and J. Grotz (eds) *The Palgrave Handbook of Volunteering, Civic Participation, and Nonprofit Associations*, Basingstoke: Palgrave Macmillan, volume 1, pp 311–329.

Anheier, H.K., Lang, M. and Toepler, S. (2019) 'Civil society in times of change: Shrinking, changing and expanding spaces and the need for new regulatory approaches', *Economics: The Open-Access, Open-Assessment E-Journal*, 13(1): 1–27.

Austin, K. and Race, M. (2022) 'What's causing flight disruption this Easter?', *BBC News*, 8 April. Available from: https://www.bbc.co.uk/news/business-61007176 [accessed 31 May 2022].

Bannister, J. and Hardill, I. (2014) *Knowledge Mobilisation and the Social Sciences: Research Impact and Engagement*, London: Routledge.

Bassel, L. and Emejulu, A. (2018) 'Caring subjects: Migrant women and the third sector in England and Scotland', *Ethnic & Racial Studies*, 41(1): 36–54.

BBC (2022) 'Who can still get free Covid tests across the UK and can I buy LFTs?', *BBC News*, 3 May. Available from: https://www.bbc.co.uk/news/health-51943612 [accessed 25 July 2022].

Bennett, E., Coule, T., Damm, C., Dayson, C., Dean, J. and Macmillan, R. (2019) 'Civil society strategy: A policy review', *Voluntary Sector Review*, 10(2): 213–223.

Benneworth, P (2006) 'The rise of the region: The English context to the raging of academic debates', in I. Hardill, P. Benneworth, M. Baker and L. Budd (eds) *The Rise of the English Regions?*, London: Routledge, pp 44–68.

Boelman, V. (2021) *Volunteering and Wellbeing in the Pandemic – Part II: Rapid Evidence Review*, Cardiff: Wales Centre for Public Policy. Available from: https://www.wcpp.org.uk/wp-content/uploads/2021/06/Volunteering-and-wellbeing-in-the-pandemic.-Part-2-Rapid-evidence-review.pdf [accessed 31 May 2022].

Bondi, L. (2014) 'Understanding feelings: Engaging with unconscious communication and embodied knowledge', *Emotion, Space and Society*, 10: 44–54.

Brewis, G., Ellis Paine, A., Hardill, I., Lindsey, R. and Macmillan, R. (2021) *Transformational Moments in Social Welfare: What Role for Voluntary Action?*, Bristol: Policy Press.

British Academy (2021) *Shaping the COVID Decade: Addressing the Long-term Societal Impacts of COVID-19*, London: British Academy. Available from: https://www.thebritishacademy.ac.uk/publications/shaping-the-covid-decade-addressing-the-long-term-societal-impacts-of-covid-19/ [accessed 31 May 2022].

Brodie, E., Hughes, T., Jochum, V., Miller, S., Ockenden, N. and Warburton, D. (2011) *Pathways through Participation: What Creates and Sustains Active Citizenship?*, London: NCVO, IVR, involve. Available from: https://www.involve.org.uk/resources/publications/project-reports/pathways-through-participation [accessed 31 May 2022].

Browne, J., Jochum, V. and Paylor, J. (2013) *The Value of Giving a Little Time: Understanding the Potential of Micro-volunteering*, London: IVR, NCVO. Available from: https://www.bl.uk/col lection-items/value-of-giving-a-little-time-understanding-the-potential-of-microvolunteering [accessed 31 May 2022].

Burchell, J., Walkley, F., Cook, J., Thiery, H., Ballantyne, E. and McNeill, J. (2020) *Report #2 Models and Frameworks for Coordinating Community Responses during COVID-19*, Sheffield: University of Sheffield.

Cabinet Office, (2018) *Civil society strategy: Building a future that works for everyone.* London: Cabinet Office.

Calvert, J. and Arbuthnott, G. (2021) *Failures of State: The Inside Story of Britain's Battle with Coronavirus*, London: Mudlark.

Chaney, P. and Williams, C. (2003) 'Getting involved: Civic and political life in Wales', in C. Williams, N. Evans and P. O'Leary (eds) *A Tolerant Nation? Exploring Ethnic Diversity in Wales*, Cardiff: University of Wales Press, pp 201–219.

Charity Commission (2021) *COVID-19 Survey 2021*, Charity Commission. Available from: https://www.gov.uk/government/ publications/charity-commission-covid-19-survey-2021 [accessed 31 May 2022].

Charity Link (2022) 'The cost of living crisis and the impact on UK charities', *Charity News Blog*, 11 May. Available from: https:// www.charitylink.net/blog/cost-of-living-crisis-impact-uk-charit ies [accessed 11 May 2022].

Cook, J., Thiery, H., Burchell, H., Walkley, F., Ballantyne, E. and McNeill, J. (2020) *Report #1 Lessons from Lockdown: Mobilising Volunteers Effectively*, report on the website of CVS Cheshire, October. Available from: https://doit.life/channels/11997/ move-findings/file/md/139216/report-1-lessons-from-lockdown [accessed 31 May 2022].

Corry, D. (2020) *Where are England's Charities?*, London: New Philanthropy Capital.

Coutts, P., Bowyer, G., Heydecker, R., Ormston, H., Pennycook, L., Thurman, B. and Wallace, J. (2020) *COVID-19 and Communities Listening Project: A Shared Response*, Dunfermline: Carnegie UK Trust. Available from: https://www.carnegieuktrust.org.uk/publi cations/covid-19-and-communities-listening-project-a-shared-response/ [accessed 31 May 2022].

Crawford, L. (2021) 'Working paper 2: What the existing research tells us', working paper on the MVAin4 project website, 30 June. Available from: https://www.mvain4.uk/resource-details/work ing-paper-2-what-the-existing-research-tells-us/ [accessed 31 May 2022].

Cretu, C. (2020) *A Catalyst for Change: What COVID-19 Has Taught Us About the Future of Local Government*, London: Nesta. Available from: https://www.nesta.org.uk/report/catalyst-cha nge/ [accessed 31 May 2022].

Curtin, M., Rendall, J.S., Roy, M.J. and Teasdale, S. (2021) *Solidarity in a Time of Crisis: The Role of Mutual Aid to the COVID-19 Pandemic*, Glasgow: Yunus Centre for Social Business and Health/ Glasgow Caledonian University.

Davies, R. (1999) *Devolution: A Process not an Event*, Cardiff: Institute of Welsh Affairs.

Davis Smith, J. (2019) *100 Years of NCVO and Voluntary Action: Idealists and Realists*, Basingstoke: Macmillan.

Dayson, C. and Damm, C. (2020) 'Re-making state-civil society relationships during the COVID 19 pandemic? An English perspective', *People, Place & Policy Online*, 14(3): 282–289.

Dayson, C., Simpson, E., Ellis-Paine, A., Gilbertson, J. and Karamade, H. (2021) 'The "resilience" of community organisations during the COVID-19 pandemic: Absorptive, adaptive and transformational capacity during a crisis response', *Voluntary Sector Review*, 12(2): 295–304.

Department for Communities (Northern Ireland) (2020a) 'COVID-19 community response plan', *Department for Communities*. Available from: https://www.nicva.org/article/dfc-covid-19-community-response-plan [accessed 30 April 2020].

Department for Communities (Northern Ireland) (2020b) *Coronavirus Protocols for Councils Who Engage Voluntary and Community Organisations in Regulated Activity with Adults*, Belfast: Department for Communities.

Department for Communities (Northern Ireland) (2020c) 'Coronavirus protocols for councils who engage voluntary and community organisations in regulated activity with adults', report, *Department for Communities*. Available from: https://www.comm unities-ni.gov.uk/sites/default/files/publications/communities/ dfc-covid-19-protocols-for-councils-voluntary-organisations.pdf [accessed 31 August 2020].

Department for Digital, Culture, Media and Sport (2021) 'Community life survey 2020/21: Volunteering and charitable giving', *gov.uk*. Available from: https://www.gov.uk/government/ statistics/community-life-survey-202021-volunteering-and-cha ritable-giving [accessed 31 May 2022].

Department for Digital, Culture, Media and Sport (2022) *Government Response to Danny Kruger MP's Report: 'Levelling Up Our Communities: Proposals for a New Social Covenant'*, London: HM Government.

Department of Education (Northern Ireland) (2020) 'C-19 guidance to volunteers in the education sector in supporting key workers and vulnerable children', *Department of Education*. Available from: https://www.education-ni.gov.uk/c-19-guidance-volunte ers-education-sector-supporting-key-workers-and-vulnerable- children [accessed 31 March 2020].

Department for Social Development (2012) *Join In, Get Involved: Build a Better Future – a Volunteering Strategy and Action Plan for Northern Ireland*, Belfast: Department for Social Development.

Donahue, K., McGarvey, A., Rooney, K. and Jochum, V. (2020) *Time Well Spent: Diversity and Volunteering, What Does Volunteer Participation Look Like*, London: NCVO.

Eden Communities Report (2021) 'The spectrum of volunteer participation', report, *Eden Project*. Available from: https://www. edenprojectcommunities.com/sites/default/files/volunteer_rep ort.pdf [accessed 31 May 2022].

Ellis Paine, A. (2020) 'Volunteering through crisis and beyond: Starting, stopping, shifting', *Rapid Research COVID-19 Briefing 5*, Local Trust. Available from: https://localtrust.org.uk/insights/research/briefing-5-rapid-research-covid-19/ [accessed 17 August 2021].

Ellis Paine, A., McCabe, A., Sugarman, W. and Leidecker, L. (2021) *Briefing 14: Community Responses to COVID-19: Sustaining Community Action*, London: Local Trust.

Emejulu, A. and Bassel, L. (2020) 'The politics of exhaustion', *City*, 24(1–2): 400–406.

ESRC (2021a) 'New ESRC COVID-19 research', *ESRC*. Available from: https://webarchive.nationalarchives.gov.uk/ukgwa/20210901104426/https://esrc.ukri.org/about-us/strategy-and-priorities/new-esrc-covid-19-research/ [accessed 8 May 2021].

ESRC (2021b) 'ESRC-funded projects addressing social science and COVID-19', *UKRI*. Available from: https://www.ukri.org/publications/esrc-funded-projects-addressing-social-science-and-covid-19/ [accessed 20 August 2021].

Flyvbjerg B. (2001) *Making Social Science Matter: Why Social Inquiry Fails and How It Can Succeed Again*, Cambridge: Cambridge University Press.

Glynos, J. and Speed, E. (2012) 'Varieties of co-production in public services: Time banks in a UK health policy context', *Critical Policy Studies*, 6(4): 402–433.

Government of Wales (2020a) 'Coronavirus (COVID-19): Support for the third sector and charities during the disruption caused by COVID-19', *Government of Wales*. Available from: https://gov.wales/coronavirus-covid-19-support-for-the-third-sector-html [accessed 31 March 2020].

Government of Wales (2020b) 'Multi-million pound boost to support volunteers and Wales' most vulnerable', *Government of Wales*. Available from: https://gov.wales/multi-million-pound-boost-to-support-volunteers-and-wales-most-vulnerable [accessed 31 March 2020].

Government of Wales (2020c) 'Volunteering during the coronavirus pandemic: How you can safely help vulnerable people during the coronavirus pandemic', *Government of Wales*. Available from: https://gov.wales/volunteering-during-coronavirus-pandemic [accessed 31 March 2020].

Gregory, D. (2018) *Skittled Out? The Collapse and Revival of England's Social Infrastructure*, London: Local Trust.

Grotz, J. (2021) 'Working paper 1: A picture is worth a thousand words', *working paper on the MVAin4 project website*, 30 June. Available from: https://www.mvain4.uk/resource-details/apictureisworthathousandwords/ [accessed 31 May 2022].

Grotz, J., Dyson, S. and Birt, L. (2020) 'Pandemic policy making: The health and wellbeing effects of the cessation of volunteering on older adults during the COVID-19 pandemic', *Quality in Ageing and Older Adults*, 21(4): 261–269.

The Guardian (2022) 'Volunteers praised for huge role in giving UK public COVID jabs', *The Guardian*, 3 January. Available from: https://www.theguardian.com/world/2022/jan/03/volunteers-praised-for-huge-role-in-giving-uk-public-covid-jabs [accessed 25 February 2022].

Hansard (2020) 'Charitable and voluntary sector volume 803: Debated on Thursday 30 April 2020', *Transcripts of the UK Government*. Available from: https://hansard.parliament.uk/lords/2020-04-30/debates/7C721552-0014-4B93-913C-A33F56ED7049/CharitableAndVoluntarySector [accessed 31 May 2022].

Hardill, I., Benneworth, P., Baker, M.W. and Budd, L.C. (eds) (2006) *The Rise of the English Regions?* London: Routledge.

Harris, M. (2020) 'Familiar patterns and news initiatives: UK civil society and the government's initial response to the COVID 19 crisis', *Nonprofit Policy Forum*, 12(1): 25–44.

Hennessy, P. (2022) *Duty of Care: Britain before and after COVID*, London: Allen Lane.

Hodgkinson, G.P., Herriot, P. and Anderson, N. (2001) 'Re-aligning the stakeholders in management research: Lessons from industrial, work and organizational psychology', *British Journal of Management*, 12: 41–48.

House of Commons Health and Social Care, and Science and Technology Committees (2021) *Coronavirus: Lessons Learned to Date*, London: House of Commons Library.

Hughes, C. (2019) 'Resisting or enabling? The roll out of neo-liberal values through the voluntary and community sector in Northern Ireland', *Critical Policy Studies*, 13(1): 61–80.

Hughes, C. and Ketola, M. (2021) *Neoliberalism and the Voluntary and Community Sector in Northern Ireland*, Bristol: Policy Press.

Kearney, J. (2001) 'The values and basic principles of volunteering: Complacency or caution?', *Voluntary Action*, 3(3): 63–86; reprinted in Davis-Smith, J. and Locke, M. (eds) (2007) *Volunteering and the Test of Time: Essays for Policy, Organisation and Research*, London: Institute for Volunteering Research.

Kendall, J. and Knapp, M. (1995) 'A loose and baggy monster: Boundaries, definitions and typologies', in J. Davis Smith, C. Rochester and R. Hedley (eds) *An Introduction to the Voluntary Sector*, London: Routledge, pp 66–95.

Knapton, S. (2022) 'Sage stands down, signifying "end of Covid pandemic" in the UK', *The Telegraph*, 4 March. Available from: https://www.telegraph.co.uk/news/2022/03/04/sage-stands-signifying-end-covid-pandemic-uk/ [accessed 31 May 2022].

Kruger, D. (2020) 'Levelling up our communities: Proposals for a new social covenant', report. Available from: https://www.dannykruger.org.uk/sites/www.dannykruger.org.uk/files/2020-09/Kruger%202.0%20Levelling%20Up%20Our%20Communities.pdf / [accessed 31 May 2021].

LGA (2020) 'Accessing support: The role of the voluntary and community sector during COVID-19', *Local Government Association*. Available from: https://www.local.gov.uk/sites/default/files/documents/Accessing%20support%20the%20role%20of%20the%20voluntary%20and%20community%20sector%20during%20COVID-19%20WEB.pdf [accessed 31 May 2022].

Macmillan, R. (2013) 'De-coupling the state and the third sector? The "Big Society" as a spontaneous order', *Voluntary Sector Review*, 4(2): 185–203.

Macmillan, R. (2020a) 'Somewhere over the rainbow: Third sector research in and beyond coronavirus', *Voluntary Sector Review*, 11(2): 129–136.

Macmillan, R. (2020b) *Briefing 3 Rapid Research. Grassroots Action: The Role of Informal Community Activity in Responding to Crises*, London: Local Trust. Available from: https://localtrust.org.uk/wp-content/uploads/2020/07/COVID-19.-Briefing-3.pdf [accessed 31 May 2022].

Macmillan, R. (2021) 'A surprising turn of events: Episodes towards a renaissance of civil society infrastructure', *People, Place and Policy*, 15(20): 57–71.

McCabe, A., Wilson, M. and Macmillan, R. (2020) *Community Resilience or Resourcefulness?*, London: Local Trust.

McCabe, A., Ellis Paine, A., Afridi, A. and Longdale, E. (2021) *Briefing 16 – Community Responses to COVID-19: Connecting Communities? How Relationships Have Mattered in Community Responses to COVID-19*, London: Local Trust.

McMullen, J. and Macmillan, R. (2021) *Stepping Up: Coordinating Local Voluntary Sector Responses to the COVID-19 Crisis*, Sheffield: Sheffield Hallam University, Centre for Regional Economic and Social Research.

Mills, S. (2013) '"An instruction in good citizenship": Scouting and the historical geographies of citizenship education', *Transactions of the Institute of British Geographers*, 38(1): 120–134.

Mills, S. and Waite, C. (2018) 'From big society to shared society? Geographies of social cohesion and encounter in the UK's National Citizen Service', *Geografiska Annaler: Series B Human Geography*, 100(2): 131–148.

National Audit Office (2020) *The supply of personal protective equipment (PPE) during the COVID-19 pandemic*, London: National Audit Office. Available from: https://www.nao.org.uk/wp-content/uploads/2020/11/The-supply-of-personal-protective-equipment-PPE-during-the-COVID-19-pandemic.pdf [accessed 23 July 2022].

National Council for Voluntary Organisations (2021) *UK Civil Society Almanac*, London: National Council of Voluntary Organisations. Available from: https://beta.ncvo.org.uk/ncvo-publications/uk-civil-society-almanac-2021/financials/income-sources/ [accessed 31 May 2022].

NHS England (2020a) '"Your NHS Needs You": NHS call for volunteer army', *NHS England*, 24 March. Available from: https://www.england.nhs.uk/2020/03/your-nhs-needs-you-nhs-call-for-volunteer-army/ [accessed 31 May 2022].

NHS England (2020b) 'Advice regarding NHS volunteers relating to COVID-19 (version 3) version 2 published', *NHS England*, 24 March, 15 May, updates to Version 3 published on 17 March 2021. Available from: https://www.england.nhs.uk/coronavirus/wp-content/uploads/sites/52/2020/04/C1139_Advice-regarding-NHS-volunteers-relating-to-COVID-19.pdf [accessed 31 May 2020].

Northern Ireland Council for Voluntary Action (2021) 'State of the sector', *Northern Ireland Council for Voluntary Action*. Available from: https://www.nicva.org/stateofthesector/income-expenditure [accessed 7 February 2022].

Office of Northern Ireland Direct Government Services (2020) 'Volunteering during the Coronavirus (COVID-19) pandemic', *ni-direct*. Available from: https://www.nidirect.gov.uk/articles/volunteering-during-coronavirus-covid-19-pandemic [accessed 1 Feb 2021].

Pape, U., Brandsen, T., Pahl, J.B., Pielin B., Baturina, D., Brookes, N., et al (2020) 'Changing policy environments in Europe and the resilience of the third sector', *Voluntas*, 31: 238–249.

Peek, N., Sujan, M. and Scott, P. (2020) 'Digital health and care in pandemic times: Impact of COVID-19', *BMJ Health & Care Informatics*, 27(1): e100166.

Rees, J. and Mullins, D. (2016) 'The third sector delivering public services: Setting out the terrain', in J. Rees and D. Mullins (eds) *The Third Sector Delivering Public Services*, Bristol: Policy Press, pp 1–19.

Roberts, P. and Baker, M.W. (2006) 'Regions and regional identity', in I. Hardill, P. Benneworth, M. Baker and L. Budd (eds) (2006) *The Rise of the English Regions?*, London: Routledge, pp 22–43.

Royal Voluntary Service (2020) *Findings: Patients Supported by the NHS Volunteer Responder Programme during COVID-19 – April to August 2020, Working Paper One*, London: Royal Voluntary Service.

Rutherford, A. and Spath, R. (2021) 'Working paper four: Volunteering in the pandemic – evidence from two UK volunteer matching services', working paper on the MVAin4 project website, 9 November. Available from: https://www.mvain4.uk/resource-details/working-paper-4-volunteering-in-the-pandemic-evidence-from-two-uk-volunteer-matching-services/ [accessed 31 May 2022].

Scottish Government (2004) 'The Civil Contingencies Act 2004 (Contingency Planning) (Scotland) Regulations 2005', *legislation.gov.uk*. Available from: https://www.legislation.gov.uk/ssi/2005/494/contents/made [accessed 28 February 2022].

Scottish Government (2019a) 'Building resilient communities: Scottish guidance on community resilience – principles, approach and good practice'. Available from: https://ready.scot/sites/default/files/2020-09/publications-preparing-scotland-building-community-resilience_.pdf [accessed 22 July 2022].

Scottish Government (2019b) 'Volunteering for all: Our national framework'. Available from: https://www.gov.scot/publications/volunteering-national-framework/ [accessed 22 July 2022].

Scottish Government (2020a) 'Supporting communities funding: Speech by Communities Secretary'. Available from: https://www.gov.scot/publications/supporting-communities-funding-statement/ [accessed 22 July 2022].

Scottish Government (2020b) 'Protecting Scotland, renewing Scotland'. Available from: https://www.gov.scot/publications/protecting-scotland-renewing-scotland-governments-programme-scotland-2020-2021/documents/ [accessed 31 May 2022].

Scottish Government (2020c) 'Coronavirus (COVID-19): Scotland's strategic framework', 23 October. Available from: https://www.gov.scot/publications/covid-19-scotlands-strategic-framework/ [accessed 31 May 2022].

Scottish Government (2020d) 'How Scotland prepares'. Available from: https://ready.scot/how-scotland-prepares [accessed 26 July 2022].

Scottish Government (2022a) 'National performance framework'. Available from: https://nationalperformance.gov.scot/ [accessed 26 July 2022].

Scottish Government (2022b) 'Scottish third sector perspectives on volunteering during COVID-19: Survey report'. Available from: https://www.gov.scot/publications/scottish-third-sector-perspectives-volunteering-during-covid-19-survey-report/ [accessed 26 July 2022].

Scottish Government (2022c) 'Scottish household survey 2020 – telephone survey: Key findings'. Available from https://www.gov.scot/publications/scottish-household-survey-2020-telephone-survey-key-findings/ [accessed 26 July 2022].

Scottish Government (2022d) 'Scotland's Volunteering Action Plan'. Available from: https://www.gov.scot/publications/scotlands-volunteering-action-plan/ [accessed 26 July 2022].

Smith, C. and Menzies, V. (2022) 'Different approaches around the UK have little overall impact', *The Times*, 24 January, p 17.

Smith, F., Timbrell, H., Woolvin, M., Muirhead, S. and Fyfe, N. (2010) 'Enlivened Geographies Enlivened geographies of volunteering: Situated, embodied and emotional practices of voluntary action', *Scottish Geographical Journal*, 126(4): 258–274.

Southby, K., South, J. and Bagnall, A.M. (2019) 'A rapid review of barriers to volunteering for potentially disadvantaged groups and implications for health inequalities', *VOLUNTAS: International Journal of Voluntary and Nonprofit Organizations*, 30(5): 907–920.

Speed, E. (2021) 'Working paper three: Preliminary analysis of policy differences across the four UK jurisdictions', *working paper on the MVAin4 project website*. Available from: https://www.mvain4.uk/resource-details/working-paper-3/ [accessed 31 May 2022].

Speed, E. (2022) 'Preliminary analysis of within case policy process across the 4 UK jurisdictions, between March 23rd 2020 and March 22nd 2021', *working paper on the MVAin4 project website*. Available from: https://www.mvain4.uk/wp-content/uploads/2022/04/Policy-Analysis-Working-Paper-5-2.pdf [accessed 31 May 2022].

Stuart, J., Kamerāde, D., Connolly, S., Ellis Paine, A., Nichols, G. and Grotz, J. (2020) *The Impacts of Volunteering on the Subjective Wellbeing of Volunteers: A Rapid Evidence Assessment*, London: What Works Centre for Wellbeing and Spirit of 2012. Available from: https://whatworkswellbeing.org/wp-content/uploads/2020/10/Volunteer-wellbeing-technical-report-Oct2020-a.pdf [accessed 31 May 2022].

Taylor, B (2015) 'How is the "killing the SNP stone dead" project going?', *BBC News*, 4 February. Available from: https://www.bbc.co.uk/news/uk-scotland-31129382 [accessed 31 May 2022].

Tiratelli, L. and Kaye, S. (2020) *Communities vs Coronavirus: The Rise of Mutual Aid*, London: New Local Government Network.

Together (2021) *Our Chance to Reconnect: Final Report of the Talk Project*, London: Together.

Tremblay, S., Castiglione, S., Audet, L-A., Desmarais, M., Horace, M. and Pelaez, S. (2021) 'Conducting qualitative research to respond to COVID-19 challenges: Reflections for the present and beyond', *International Journal of Qualitative Research*, 20: 1–8.

UK Government (2020a) 'Coronavirus: How to help safely'. Available from: https://www.gov.uk/coronavirus-volunteering/ [accessed 26 July 2022].

UK Government (2020b) 'Coronavirus (COVID-19) guidance for the charity sector', 7 April, last updated 25 March 2022. Available from: https://www.gov.uk/guidance/coronavirus-covid-19-guidance-for-the-charity-sector [accessed 31 April 2020].

UK Government (2020c) 'Financial support for voluntary, community and social enterprise (VCSE) organisations to respond to coronavirus (COVID-19)', 20 May, last updated 10 March 2022. Available from: https://www.gov.uk/guidance/financial-support-for-voluntary-community-and-social-enterprise-vcse-organisations-to-respond-to-coronavirus-covid-19 [accessed 31 April 2020].

UK Government (2020d) 'NHS volunteers extend support to frontline health and social care staff', 6 June. Available from: https://www.gov.uk/government/news/nhs-volunteers-ext end-support-to-frontline-health-and-social-care-staff [accessed 07 June 2020].

UK Health Security Agency (2022) 'Prevalence of COVID-19 remains at high levels across the country', 6 April. Available from: https://www.gov.uk/government/news/prevalence-of-covid-19-remains-at-high-levels-across-the-country [accessed 26 July 2022].

UKRI (2020) 'Get funding for ideas that address COVID-19'. Available from: https://www.ukri.org/opportunity/get-fund ing-for-ideas-that-address-covid-19/ [accessed 31 May 2022].

Volunteer Now (2021) 'Volunteering during the pandemic and beyond: A Northern Ireland perspective'. Available from: https://www.volunteernow.co.uk/app/uploads/2021/04/QUB-COVID-Volunteering-Report-Mar2021-2.pdf [accessed 7 February 2022].

Volunteer Scotland (2019) '2018 formal and informal volunteering – hours and economic value'. Available from https://www.volunteerscotland.net/for-organisations/research-and-evaluation/publications/scottish-household-survey-cross-sectional-analysis/ (see 'Formal and Informal volunteering 2018' under 'Related Downloads: 2018') [accessed 10 December 2021].

Volunteer Scotland (2020a) 'Impact of COVID-19 on volunteering participation in Scotland'. Available from: https://www.volunt eerscotland.net/for-organisations/research-and-evaluation/publi cations/covid-19-research/impact-of-covid-19-on-volunteering-participation-in-scotland/ [accessed 26 July 2022].

Volunteer Scotland (2020b) 'TSI Scotland network survey on the "impact of COVID-19 on the third sector in Scotland" – Volunteer Scotland's analysis: June and October 2020'. Available from: https://www.volunteerscotland.net/for-organisations/research-and-evaluation/publications/covid-19-research/impact-of-covid-19-on-the-third-sector-in-scotland/ [accessed 26 July 2022].

Volunteer Scotland (2021) 'OSCR's surveys on the impact of COVID-19 on Scot-land's charities – Volunteer Scotland's supplementary analysis: February 2021 and May 2021'. Available from: https://www.volunteerscotland.net/for-organisations/research-and-evaluation/publications/covid-19-research/impact-of-covid-19-on-scotlands-charities/ [accessed 26 July 2022].

Volunteer Scotland (2022) *The Road to Recovery: Lessons Learned from Scotland's Response to COVID-19*, Stirling: Volunteer Scotland. Available from: https://www.volunteerscotland.net/for-organisations/research-and-evaluation/publications/covid-19-research/the-road-to-recovery/ [accessed 26 July 2022].

VSSN (2020a) 'Covid-19 research repository'. Available from: https://www.vssn.org.uk/covid-19-and-voluntary-action-research-repository-projects/ [accessed 31 May 2022].

VSSN (2020b) '2020 VSVR online conference – session videos'. Available from: https://www.vssn.org.uk/2020-vsvr-online-conference-session-videos/ [accessed 31 May 2022].

WCVA (2019) *Cyllid cynaliadwy i'r trydydd sector / Sustainable Funding for the Third Sector*, Cardiff: WCVA. Available from: https://wcva.cymru/wp-content/uploads/2019/11/sustainable_funding_for_the_third_sector_report__4_.pdf [accessed 31 May 2022].

WCVA (2020) 'WCVA written evidence', Welsh Parliament, online report. Available from: https://business.senedd.wales/documents/s108218/COV%20VS%2008%20-%20WCVA.pdf [Accessed 20 July 2022].

Weiss, C.H. (1972) *Evaluation Research: Methods for Assessing Program Effectiveness*, Englewood Cliffs: Prentice Hall.

Welsh Government (2014) *Third Sector Scheme*, Cardiff: Welsh Government. Available from: https://gov.wales/sites/default/files/publications/2019-01/third-sector-scheme-2014.pdf [accessed 31 May 2022].

Welsh Parliament Equality, Local Government, and Communities Committee (2021) *Impact of COVID-19 on the Voluntary Sector in Wales*, Cardiff: Welsh Parliament. Available from: https://senedd.wales/media/d4jh52zz/cr-ld14075-e.pdf [accessed 31 May 2022].

Williams, C.C. (2003) 'Developing community participation in deprived neighbourhoods: A critical evaluation of the third sector approach', *Space and Polity*, 7(1): 65–73.

Williams, C.C. (2011) 'Socio-spatial variations in community self help: A total social organisation of labour perspective', *Social Policy and Society*, 10(3): 365–78.

Wilson, M., McCabe, A. and Macmillan, R. (2020a) *Briefing 4 Rapid Research COVID-19. Blending Formal and Informal Community Responses*, London: Local Trust. Available from: https://localtrust.org.uk/wp-content/uploads/2020/08/COVID-19-BRIEFING-4.pdf [accessed 31 May 2022].

Wilson, M., McCabe, A., Macmillan, R. and Ellis Paine, A. (2020b) *Briefing 8 Rapid Research COVID-19. Community Responses to COVID-19: The Role and Contribution of Community-led Infrastructure*, London: Local Trust. Available from: https://localtrust.org.uk/wp-content/uploads/2020/12/COVID-19-Briefing-8.pdf [accessed 31 May 2022].

WISERD (2020) 'Wales Institute of Social & Economic Research data written evidence for Welsh Parliament', online report. Available from: https://business.senedd.wales/documents/s108628/COV%20VS%2020%20-%20Wales%20Institute%20for%20Social%20and%20Economic%20Research%20and%20Data%20WISERD.pdf [accessed 20 July 2022].

Woolvin, M. and Hardill, I. (2013) 'Localism, voluntarism and devolution: Experiences, opportunities and challenges in a changing policy context', *Local Economy*, 28(3): 275–290.

Woolvin, M. and Harper, H. (2015) *Volunteering from 'Below the Radar'. Informal Volunteering in Deprived Urban Scotland: Research Summary*, Stirling: Volunteer Scotland. Available from: https://www.volunteerscotland.net/media/624210/mw_phd_summary_30_07_15.pdf [accessed 31 May 2022].

Woolvin, M., Mills, S., Hardill, I. and Rutherford, A. (2015) 'Devolved responses to national challenges? Voluntarism and devolution in England, Wales and Scotland', *Geographical Journal*, 181(1): 38–46.

Wyler, S. (2020) *Community responses in times of crisis: Glimpses into the past, present and future*, London: Local Trust and Big Local. Available from: https://localtrust.org.uk/wp-content/uploads/2020/05/22040_Community-responses-in-times-of-crisis_on line_lr.pdf [accessed 31 May 2022].

Yang, R., Harvey, C., Mueller, F. and Maclean, M. (2021) 'The role of mediators in diffusing the community foundation model of philanthropy', *Nonprofit and Voluntary Sector Quarterly*, 50(5): 1–24.

ZOE COVID Study (2020) 'ZOE COVID Symptom Study proves the power of citizen science', 4 December. Available from: https://covid.joinzoe.com/post/covid-power-of-citizen-science [accessed 10 April 2022].

Index

References to figures and images
appear in *italic* type; those in **bold** type refer to tables.

A

Acheson, N. 62, 64, 65, 139
Aguirre, B.E. 142
Anheier, H.K. 63
Arbuthnott, G. 2
'The Arches' project *1*
austerity 43, 106, 108, 109, 119,
    126, 146
Austin, K. 131

B

Baker, M.W. 4
Bannister, J. 8, 12
Bassel, L. 119, 124, 125
Be Collective 9, 14, 66, 70,
    73, 134
Bennett, E. 45
Benneworth, P. 4
Big Lottery 139, 146
Big Society 23, 43, 146
Blair, T. 4
blended approaches/activities 107,
    120–121, 142, 146
Boelman, V. 106
borders 143
Brewis, G. 43, 44, 49, 145
Brexit 110–111
British Academy 142
Brodie, E. 145
Burchell, J. 36, 49

C

call for evidence 14–15
Calvert, J. 2
carers 113–117
Chaney, P. 111
charitable income 108, 110
Charity Commission Northern
    Ireland (CCNI) 64, 147
Charity Link 141
#CharitySoWhite 57, 147
Chester City football ground 143
citizen response 27–34, 141
Civil Contingencies Act 2004
    (Contingency Planning)
    (Scotland) Regulations
    2005 87
civil contingencies planning 77–78
civil society 11
Civil Society Strategy 2018 23,
    45, 147
Clwb Rygbi Nant Conxy *105*
co-production 9, 12, 133, 147
Coalition government 11, 43
collaboration 35, 36, 133,
    137–138
  England 49–52, 57, 58
  Scotland 99
communities of place 138
community 147–148
community development 64, 65,
    75, 77, 78, 79

community engagement 101
Community Life Survey 27
community resilience 87
Conservative governments 11, 43
Cook, J. 142
Corry, D. 43
Council for Voluntary
    Services 148
County Voluntary Councils
    (CVCs) 11, 106, 107, 112,
    116, 148
Coutts, P. 37, 41
COVID-19 2–4
    ambiguities of
        devolution 142–144
    citizen response 27–34, 141
    embracing living with *128*
    emergency legislation 129
    expected responses 99–100
    infection levels 130
    legacy on voluntary action 142
    organisational response 34–38
    public health responses 20–21
      voluntary action policy
        analysis 21–27
    Scottish timeline *84*
    timeline across UK nations **6–7**
    unexpected responses 101–102
Crawford, L. 15
Cretu, C. 36
Curtin, M. 90

D

Damm, C. 41, 44
data collection 12, 133–134, 136
Davies, R. 5
Davis Smith, J. 2, 10, 139
Dayson, C. 41, 44
Department for Communities,
    Northern Ireland 24,
    148–149
Department for Digital, Culture,
    Media and Sport 27, 33, 58,
    59, 60, 149
Department of Business, Energy
    and Industrial Strategy 148
devolution 2, 3, 4–8, 140,
    142–144
digital deprivation 120

digital exclusion 57
digital inequalities 36
digital platform operators 9, 14
digital technologies 35, 36, 92,
    101, 145
disabled volunteers 32, *33*
discourse analysis 13, 18, 149
Donahue, K. 36, 57

E

Economic and Social Research
    Council (ESRC) 3–4, 8, 12,
    82–83, 132, 133, 149
Eden Communities Report 77
Ellis Paine, A. 2, 37, 48, 54, 56,
    139, 142
Emejulu, A. 119, 124, 125
emergency leadership group 75
emergency legislation 129
emergency planning 121–122
emergency preparedness
    groups 150–151
    see also Voluntary and
        Community Sector
        Emergencies Partnership
England 40–60
    government engagement 141
    infrastructure 139
    pandemic timeline **6–7**
    partial decoupling 8
    sampling strategies 16
    voluntary action policy 22–24,
        27, 44–45
    voluntary sector
      in 2020 43–45
      future of 55–59
      in the pandemic 45–55
    volunteering rates 27–28
Equality, Local Government, and
    Communities Committee,
    Wales 111
EU funding 110–111
exhaustion 71, 119
expected responses 99–100

F

financial barriers 124
firebreak 113, 149
Flyvbjerg, B. 8, 9

food parcels *61*
formal volunteering 27–28, 29, 33, 137, 157
  England 42
  Scotland 85, 89–90, 102–103
funding
  England 43, 51
  Northern Ireland 65
  research project 3–4, 133
  Scotland 96, 99
  Wales 109, 110–111, 125
  ZOE COVID Study 130
furlough 31, 37, 136, 149
  England 46–47, 49, 56
  Northern Ireland 71, 73
  Scotland 96
  Wales 112, 123, 126

G

Gateshead 139
Glynos, J. 9, 12, 133
Good Friday Agreement 4, 8, 80, 140, 150
GoodSam 52, 150
Government of Wales Act 2006 108
Gregory, D. 58
Gross Domestic Product (GDP) 107, 150
Grotz, J. 10, 37
Guardian 53

H

Hardill, I. 3, 4, 8, 12
Harper, H. 77
Harris, M. 74
health policy 2
  see also policy analysis; public health responses
Heneghan, Prof. C. 130
Hennessy, P. 2
Hodgkinson, G.P. 9
Home-Start Bolton *128*
Hughes, C. 4, 8, 62, 65

I

inclusive volunteering 102
industrial heritage site 112–113

infection levels 130
informal volunteering 27–28, 34, 157
  England 42
  Northern Ireland 68, 70, 73, 74
  Scotland 85, 89–90, 90–91, 94, 100, 103
  Wales 125
  see also mutual aid
infrastructure 37, 131, 138–140
  England 41, 43, 53, 55, 58–59, 139
infrastructure organisations 11, 16, 139, 155–156
  England 42, 47, 48, 49–50, 51–52, 54
  Northern Ireland 71–72, 75, 77
  Scotland 83, 87–88, 90, 91, 93–96, 100, 102, 103
  Wales 106, 123
interdisciplinary approach 13
interviews 17, 67, 107

J

'Just do it' attitude 102

K

Kaye, S. 35–36, 47
Kearney, J. 10
Kendall, J. 11
Ketola, M. 4, 8, 62, 65
Knapp, M. 11
Knapton, S. 130
Kruger Review 22–23

L

Labour Manifesto 1992 4
leadership 98
Lessons Learnt (House of Commons, 2021) 54
levelling up 58–59, 60, 150
'Levelling up our communities' (Kruger, 2020) 22–23
Local Government Association (LGA) 22
Local Resilience Forums 138, 150–151

Local Resilience Partnerships 44, 98, 150–151
Local Trust 139, 151
lockdown 2, 3, **6**, 137, 151
  England 47
  Northern Ireland 67
  Scotland 90, 91
  Wales 112–113, 117
lockdown volunteers 31–32
loneliness 93

M

Macmillan, R. 8, 43, 44, 49, 51, 139
mass volunteering programmes 52–55
McCabe, A. 41, 49, 57
McMullen, J. 51
media 144
mental health 93, 118
Menzies, V. 8
micro-charities 108
micro volunteering 139, 151
Mills, S. 124
mixed-methods approach 13
'Mobilising Voluntary Action Across the UK' research study 82–83
MOVE project 36
mutual aid 2, 35–36, 151–152
  England 47, 48, 50
  Scotland 90, 101

N

National Citizenship Scheme 124
National Council for Voluntary Organisations 57, 152
National Voluntary Sector Coordination (NVC) Hub 138
New Labour 4, 11, 43, 65
NHS Volunteer Responders Programme 52, 53, 54, 152
Northern Ireland 61–80
  changes in volunteering responses *69*
  Department for Communities 148–149
  devolution 4, 8, 143

infrastructure 139
pandemic timeline **6–7**
policy analysis 140
sampling strategies 16
voluntary action policy analysis 24–25, 27
voluntary sector
  in 2020 63–66
  future of 76–78
  in the pandemic 66–75
Northern Ireland Council for Voluntary Action 64, 66
Northern Ireland Volunteering Strategy 10

O

Office of the Scottish Charity Regulator 91, 152
online activities 120
online support 113–117
online surveys 16–17, 67, 133
organisational response 34–38
outsourcing 62, 64

P

pandemic timeline across UK nations **6–7**
Pape, U. 63
partnership working *see* collaboration
partnerships 79, 99, 137
  see also Local Resilience Partnerships; Third Sector Partnership Council (TSPC); Voluntary Sector Resilience Partnership
Peek, N. 31
Pitkeathley, Baroness 145
policy *see* health policy; public policy; voluntary action policy; volunteering policy, Scotland
policy analysis 13–14, 21–27, 140–141
politics of exhaustion 119
public health responses 20–21
  voluntary action policy analysis 21–27
  see also policy analysis

public policy 4–8
  see also policy analysis

R

Race, M. 131
Republic of Ireland 143
research analysis 15, 34–38
research ethics 133, 152
research project
  approach and methods 11–17
  in context of a
      pandemic 132–135
  funding 3–4, 133
  key findings 135–141
  scope and definitions 8–11
resilience partnerships *see* Local
      Resilience Partnerships;
      Voluntary Sector
      Resilience Partnership
resilience planning 98
  see also Third Sector
      Resilience Fund
resilience policy, Scotland 86–88
resilience response 93–94
Road to Recovery, The (Volunteer
      Scotland) 82–83, 104
Roberts, P. 4
Robertson, G. 5
Routemap to Improvement,
      Scotland 97
Royal Voluntary Service
      (RVS) 52, 53, 54, 152
Royal Voluntary Service
      volunteer *40*
Rutherford, A. 29, 66–67, 68,
      70, 73

S

sampling strategies 16
Scientific Advisory Group for
      Emergencies (SAGE) 130
Scotland 81–104
  COVID-19 timeline *84*
  devolution 4, 5
  infrastructure 139–140
  National Voluntary Sector
      Coordination (NVC)
      Hub 138

pandemic timeline **6–7**
policy analysis 140, 141
Routemap to Improvement 97
voluntary action policy
      analysis 25, 27
voluntary sector
  before COVID-19 84–88
  future of 96–103
  in the pandemic 88–96
  volunteering rates 28
Scotland Cares 95–96, 100
'Scotland's Volunteering Action
      Plan' (Scottish Government,
      2022) 86, 98, 104
Scottish Council for Voluntary
      Organisations (SCVO) 82,
      83, 88, 95, 140, 152
Scottish Government response
      93–94, 95–96, 103, 139
Scottish Household Survey
      (SHS) 85, 89, 153
Scottish National Party (SNP) 5
shielding 2, 70, 90, 131, 136, 153
small charities 108
Smith, C. 8
social infrastructure 58
societal needs 100
Southby, K. 57
Spath, R. 29, 66–67, 70, 73
Speed, E. 9, 12, 64, 68, 133
St John Ambulance 54
Stuart, J. 12
surveys 14–17, 41–42, 67,
      106–107, 133, 134–135
  see also Community Life Survey;
      Scottish Household Survey
      (SHS)

T

Taylor, B. 5
Team Kinetic 9, 14, 134
@ThatsDevolved 144
Theory of Change 12–13, 132
third sector 11, 153
Third Sector Interfaces (TSI) 11, 82,
      83, 91, 98, 99, 139–140, 153
Third Sector Organisations
      (TSOs) 87, 91, 93, 96,
      103, 153

Third Sector Partnership Council
(TSPC) 108, 126, 153–154
Third Sector Resilience Fund 26
Third Sector Scheme (Welsh
Government 2014) 109
Third Sector Unit 82, 140
Tiratelli, L. 35–36, 47
Together 46
training 99–100
Tremblay, S. 133
TSI Scotland Network 91, 99,
100, 140, 154

U

UK Research and Innovation
(UKRI) 3, 145, 154
unexpected responses 101–102

V

vaccination volunteering
scheme 52–53, 54, 138
Vision for Volunteering 58,
154
voluntary action 10, 122–125,
131–132, 141–144, 154
see also volunteering
voluntary action policy 21–27,
44–45, 65
voluntary action policy-making 3
voluntary action research project
approach and methods 11–17
in context of a
pandemic 132–135
funding 3–4, 133
key findings 135–141
scope and definitions 8–11
voluntary activity /
participation 112–119,
114–115, 122–125
see also volunteer registrations;
volunteering rates
voluntary and community
organisations (VCOs) 106,
109, 112, 117, 118–119, 120,
124, 154–155
Voluntary and Community
Sector Emergencies
Partnership 51, 155

voluntary and community sector
(VCS) 50, 87, 136, 155
voluntary, community and social
enterprise sector 155
voluntary sector 11
England
in 2020 43–45
future of 55–59
in the pandemic 45–55
Northern Ireland
in 2020 63–66
future of 76–78
in the pandemic 66–75
Scotland
before COVID-19 84–88
future of 96–103
in the pandemic 88–96
Wales 105–127
in 2020 107–111
lessons for the future 120–125
in the pandemic 111–119
voluntary sector infrastructure
organisations *see*
infrastructure organisations
Voluntary Sector Resilience
Partnership 87
Voluntary Sector Review 3, 132
Voluntary Sector Studies Network
(VSSN) 3, 132
Volunteer Bikers NI *19*
Volunteer Edinburgh's Community
Taskforce volunteers *81*
volunteer involving organisations
(VIOs) 2, 82, 91–93, 102,
103, 112–113, 156
Volunteer Ireland 143
Volunteer Now 66, 70, 143, 156
volunteer profiles 31–32, 47
disabled volunteers 32, *33*
volunteer registrations *30*
Volunteer Scotland 141, 156
financial value of
volunteering 85
formal volunteering 103
government funding 96
resilience planning 87, 88, 94
Road to Recovery 82–83, 104
Scotland Cares 95
volunteer involving organisations
(VIOs) 91, 92, 93

volunteering 156
  dynamics of 27–34
  formal 27–28, 29, 33, 137, 157
    England 42
    Scotland 85, 89–90, 102–103
  inclusive 102
  informal 27–28, 34, 157
    England 42
    Northern Ireland 68, 70,
      73, 74
    Scotland 85, 89–90, 90–91, 94,
      100, 103
    Wales 125
    see also mutual aid
  recognition 101–102, 142
'Volunteering during the
    Coronavirus (COVID-
    19) pandemic' (Office of
    Northern Ireland Direct
    Government Services,
    2020) 24–25
'Volunteering for all' (Scottish
    Government 2019) 104
volunteering policy, Scotland
    85–86, 98
volunteering rates
  England 27–28
  Scotland 28, 85, 88–90, 95,
    103
  Wales 107
  see also voluntary activity
    / participation;
    volunteer registrations
volunteering responses Northern
    Ireland *69*
volunteers 135–137, 156
  see also volunteer profiles

W

Waite, C. 124
Wales
  additional research questions 15
  communities 138
  County Voluntary Councils
    (CVCs) 11
  devolution 4, 5, 143–144
  pandemic timeline **6–7**
  policy analysis 140, 141
  typology of voluntary
    activity **114–115**
  voluntary action policy
    analysis 26–27
  voluntary sector 105–127
    in 2020 107–111
    lessons for the future 120–125
    in the pandemic 111–119
Wales Council for Voluntary
    Action (WCVA) 26, 107,
    108–109, 110, 111, 157
Weiss, C.H. 12, 132
Welsh Government 108–109
Williams, C. 111
Williams, C.C. 77
Wilson, M. 37
women of colour 119
women's welfare 118
Woolvin, M. 3, 5, 8, 77, 132, 140
Wyler, S. 37

Y

Yang, R. 133

Z

ZOE COVID Study 130

Printed and bound by CPI Group (UK) Ltd, Croydon, CR0 4YY

13/04/2025

14656584-0004